Know When To Break The First Rule

CREATING A CULTURE OF CAN DO IN A CAN'T DO ENVIRONMENT

Joe McConnell

authorHOUSE

AuthorHouse™
1663 Liberty Drive
Bloomington, IN 47403
www.authorhouse.com
Phone: 1-800-839-8640

© 2014 Joe McConnell. All rights reserved.

No part of this book may be reproduced, stored in a retrieval system, or transmitted by any means without the written permission of the author.

Published by AuthorHouse 10/27/2015

ISBN: 978-1-4969-0849-0 (sc)
ISBN: 978-1-4969-0848-3 (hc)
ISBN: 978-1-4969-0847-6 (e)

Library of Congress Control Number: 2014907873

Print information available on the last page.

Any people depicted in stock imagery provided by Thinkstock are models, and such images are being used for illustrative purposes only.
Certain stock imagery © Thinkstock.

This book is printed on acid-free paper.

Because of the dynamic nature of the Internet, any web addresses or links contained in this book may have changed since publication and may no longer be valid. The views expressed in this work are solely those of the author and do not necessarily reflect the views of the publisher, and the publisher hereby disclaims any responsibility for them.

I only have two rules.
The first rule: never give a customer a free drink.
The second rule: know when to break the first rule.
—Restaurant owner to his newly hired bartender

Table of Contents

Introduction—Can Do versus Can't Do 1

Chapter One —The Birth of a Service Vision 7
Chapter Two —Creating a Nonnegotiable Service Vision 20
Chapter Three —Establishing Nonnegotiable Hiring Standards 33
Chapter Four —Re-Recruiting Your Best Employees through
                 Ownership and Empowerment 50
Chapter Five —Leadership: Holding Yourself to Nonnegotiable
                 Standards 62
Chapter Six —"Can You Believe This?" Utilizing Everyday
                 Experiences to Enhance Your Brand 68
Chapter Seven —Avoiding Self-Sabotage 79
Chapter Eight —Putting Your Clients First 86
Chapter Nine —Remaining True to Your Vision 95

Final Chapter—The Beginning 99

Introduction
CAN DO VERSUS CAN'T DO

> In the middle of difficulty lies opportunity.
> —Albert Einstein

All businesses have rules in place to ensure a safe and honest environment. There are also rules in place to ensure profitability. Unfortunately, some rules result in client dissatisfaction. My eighty-three-year-old mother recently bought her first computer. Embracing new technology at eighty-three was cause for celebration, or so you would think. When she called her cable provider to request an Internet connection, she mentioned this provider's advertisements for a first-year price special. The offer of ninety-nine dollars per month was a bundled price that included television, phone, and Internet. She was advised that because she was an existing customer, she was not eligible for the special offer. She pointed out that for the past several years, she had been paying more than one hundred dollars for television and phone service. In addition, she had never been late with a payment. She was, in fact, a loyal customer. By the end of the conversation, she was told again that the special price was for new customers only. That was the rule.

It is absurd for any organization to create rules that encourage client defection. It is my hope that this book will empower you to break some of your own rules and create an atmosphere that will enhance your clients' experiences and encourage client loyalty. Are you doing everything you can to ensure a positive customer experience? Do some of your policies put your customers in a negative emotional state? Perhaps it is time for you to break some rules. This book will assist you in creating the policies and practices that are essential to building a customer-centric organization.

We have all heard someone share a customer service experience. Perhaps we have shared a few of our own. Often, these experiences begin with a problem, which is what makes these stories compelling. We find ourselves drawn in by these narratives because there are only two possible finales: pleasure or pain. Regardless of the outcome, these stories are told over and over again. In some instances, they become folklore and are passed from generation to generation. We all know someone who will only drive a specific make of car or will never shop at a specific store, usually because of an experience that had occurred years ago. I can recall a story of someone who refused to shop at a specific department store because, ten years prior, his mother had been mistreated. I knew of another family who only drove Ford vehicles because GM had sold Grandpa a lemon and refused to provide a replacement. As businesspeople, we possess the ability to create memorable customer experiences. How your customers remember you and your business will determine the ending to their story, or should I say *your* story. You own your customer's story because your customer's story is your brand.

Most organizations strive to provide their customers with exemplary service, but they don't always succeed. It is impossible to satisfy every customer, but it is imperative that you use every means available to limit any negative customer experiences. Common sense tells us that a positive customer experience will help enhance your brand, but most organizations miss the opportunities that lie within a bad customer experience. Dynamic business leaders provide their employees with the autonomy to turn a negative customer experience into an enduring, positive experience. It is critical that everyone within your organization recognize the opportunities to exceed client expectations. This single quality will separate your organization from your competition. This book will provide you with the strategies required to build an airtight, customer-centric environment that will guarantee consistent, positive customer experiences. This book also includes many customer service stories that you should find both entertaining and educational.

I will complete this introduction with the customer service story that became the impetus for this book. On the same day that these events took place, my cousin and I had discussed the diminishment of customer service standards. The events that followed were compelling enough for me to stay up that same evening until four in the morning in order to build the outline for this book. I will now share with you that very ironic experience.

Last year, I visited my cousin in San Francisco. My visits always include an overnight trip to Napa and Sonoma. On our ride up to wine country, I suggested that we dine at Tra Vigne; a few years earlier, my son and I were so impressed by our experience at Tra Vigne that we continued to talk about it for months afterward. The impression was lasting enough for me to suggest that we visit Tra Vigne on our first night in Napa. The experience that night was wonderful. Our waiter was personable, knowledgeable, and engaging. We shared a few courses and everything was plated separately in the kitchen. Questions regarding the wine list were answered intelligently, and a few brief anecdotes were shared regarding vineyards and varietals. For more than two hours, we sat and enjoyed a meal as memorable and satisfying as the one I had shared years before with my son.

After dinner, we decided that we would stop for dessert at Mustards Grill, an equally venerable dining destination also in Napa. We saw it as an opportunity to enjoy two fine-dining experiences on the same night. When our waiter approached to take our dessert order, we told him of our plans to stop at Mustards Grill. He thought it was a wonderful idea and offered directions and suggested a few of his favorite desserts at Mustards Grill. We paid the bill and left a hearty tip. As we walked out, the maitre d' handed us a copy of MapQuest directions to Mustards Grill. Everyone at Tra Vigne had a can-do attitude, and we departed feeling wowed.

We found Mustards without any trouble and walked inside; we were still riding the positive wave of our Tra Vigne experience. When we walked into Mustards, our wave went flat. Our can-do experience became a chorus of can't do. The door hadn't closed behind us before the maitre d' informed us that they were closed. How, we asked, was this possible considering the parking lot was almost full? "We're closing," he said. How can that be, we asked, considering that food was being served to the tables right in front of us? "The kitchen is closing," he snapped. I thought it best to start again. After all, it might have been a crazy night and the maitre d' and wait staff could've been exhausted.

"Please understand, we only want dessert and coffee," I offered in an even and empathetic tone.

"The kitchen is closing," he said as food continued to be delivered to the tables.

"We don't even want a table. We'll sit at the bar and have dessert. I understand that your apple crisp is wonderful," I offered in a complimentary tone. At this point, I thought it best not to let him know that the waiter at Tra Vigne recommended the apple crisp.

"I've already told you, the kitchen is closing," he snapped.

"What happens to all these folks who are currently eating—aren't many of them going to order dessert?" I asked. I was prepared for a brusque retort, and I wasn't disappointed. The maitre d's face contorted into a toothy snarl as he hissed, "We're closed."

The moment dripped with irony as my cousin and I looked at each other in amazement and walked out. We had both experienced, within an hour, the opposite extremes of can do and can't do. We have told this story many times, both as an endorsement of Tra Vigne and as an example of profoundly poor customer service.

We can look at these two very different experiences and dissect them in an effort to determine their strengths and failures, but that would be too elementary an exercise. It is quite obvious that the staff at Tra Vigne was skilled and adept in creating a memorable customer experience. The fact that they were gracious enough to support our desire to visit a competitor is truly amazing and created a lasting impression. Mustards Grill failed by creating a negative lasting impression.

Everyone knows the difference between a superior customer experience and a substandard customer experience. The one thing they share in common is that both experiences are talked about, usually with passion. The language, however, is quite different; the wowed customer speaks in glowing, enthusiastic terms, while the disappointed or underwhelmed customer speaks in vitriolic terms. I have assisted Tra Vigne in gaining more business, while few, if any, of my friends will ever step inside Mustards Grill.

The purpose of this book is to look deeply into what constitutes an unforgettable customer experience. Every day, we are provided with opportunities to exceed our customers' expectations. Do you and your team pounce on those opportunities? If you don't, you are missing out on opportunities to drive sales and revenue through client retention and word-of-mouth advertising. By recognizing and seizing these opportunities, your organization can increase profits without incurring any additional cost. Let us assume the maitre d' at Mustards Grill was correct and the kitchen was indeed ready to close. Now also imagine if the maitre d', after witnessing our disappointment, asked us to wait a moment while he went in to ask the kitchen if two more desserts could be prepared. How different would our experience have been if he returned to seat us at a table and personally provide the dessert selections? What would that have cost? Nothing! What it could have bought was a memorable experience, which we would have shared with our friends and family.

In this book, I will discuss ways in which you can build an enduring organizational philosophy around a culture of service. You will discover ways in which everyone in your organization will view problems as opportunities to create lasting impressions and long-lasting client relationships. Your customer's reality is your brand. If you make your brand dynamic and exciting, your customers will carry your message and drive your sales.

Chapter One
THE BIRTH OF A SERVICE VISION

I was fortunate enough to learn the value of a superior customer experience early in life. My first formal job was delivering newspapers after school. I quickly noticed that the guys making the most money all did the same thing when it rained: they purchased plastic bags for their newspapers. This was an additional cost that most of the delivery boys didn't wish to incur. I quickly learned that dry papers led to bigger tips. The bags cost a penny apiece and were sold in one-hundred-piece lots. A dollar was a lot of money (the newspaper itself only cost seven cents), and it took an additional half hour to fold and insert the papers into the bags before loading up the bicycle baskets and heading out, but the rewards of providing a superior service were substantial. I had taken over a route from someone who apparently never thought to keep his papers dry on rainy days, and by exceeding expectations, I found myself being well tipped. I also began receiving referrals. As I advanced to jobs where I had to punch a clock and work within established rules, I was amazed to see that most companies took their customers for granted.

At the age of seventeen, I was offered a job at Bloomingdale's where my rudimentary understanding of the power of service was validated. I quickly learned about Bloomingdale's generous return policy. My first introduction to the policy was early in my tenure, when a customer asked to return a swimsuit. This occurred in September, and the swimsuit was faded by months of sunshine and chlorinated pool water. When I approached my manager with the customer's absurd request, I was surprised when she instructed me to take it back and issue a full credit. When I protested and pointed out that the swimsuit had been used for the entire season, my manager repeated her instruction and suggested that I not keep the customer waiting.

Later that same day, my manager invited me to join her for coffee in the employees' cafeteria. Over a cup of coffee and a slice of pie, she explained the Bloomingdale's policy. In essence, Bloomingdale's was focused on the "customer's reality." That reality, she explained, is Bloomingdale's brand. Some customers take advantage of the liberal return policy, but by and large, most customers are honest and straightforward when it comes to returning merchandise. It wasn't worth risking Bloomingdale's brand by arguing over a $37.50 credit.

I immediately saw the value in this policy. Years earlier, when I had absorbed a cost in order to keep my customers' papers dry, I had been rewarded with bigger tips and additional customers. Without knowing it at the time, I had established my own brand, which was built on service and care. Bloomingdale's was enhancing its brand by absorbing the cost associated to returned merchandise. The store's customers had grown to expect superior service and Bloomingdale's remained committed to those standards long after the original purchase.

Those positive experiences helped establish the foundation of my own nonnegotiable standards. Equally important were the negative experiences, which, I quickly came to realize, outnumbered the positive experiences. By paying attention to your competitors' weaknesses, you can look for ways to exceed client expectations. This is the good news if you're looking to differentiate yourself within your marketplace. The field of play quickly shrinks when you become a customer-focused organization. Your competitors' weaknesses are the soft spots that you can exploit. Let's take a look at a few common customer service failures that represent much of what we experience every day.

I will take these real-life examples and dissect them so that you can see ways in which you can take both your own and your competitors' service voids and fill them with memorable customer experiences. Within your marketplace, your customer base is underwhelmed by similarity; they have grown accustomed to a bland experience, and it won't take much to differentiate your organization from the competition. However, you must be resolute in maintaining those differences.

The first two examples involve long-term client/vendor relationships. Many organizations tend to forget long-term clients in their effort to capture new clients. Although it costs, on average, five times as much to secure a new client than it does to keep an existing one, most organizations confuse customer loyalty with customer complacency. They assume that a client will remain a client strictly out of habit and convenience. While this, can be true at times, do you really want your clients to feel begrudged and resigned?

My first example involves a local dry-cleaning service. For twelve years, I have utilized a small dry cleaner in my neighborhood, and like most people, I've experienced a few disappointments, but I chose to ignore those occasional failures in favor of convenience—this shop is only two blocks from my home. On this particular day, I removed the plastic wrapper from my shirt and noticed that the color had been bleached out on both sleeves. I should point out that this was one of four golf shirts that I had bought the previous year, and I spent a higher than usual amount on these shirts because they fit me well and were well constructed. Usually, I would wash a golf shirt at home, but because I considered these shirts special (they were, by my standards, expensive), I decided I would do my best to extend their lives by having them professionally laundered. A few days later, I returned to the dry cleaner with my ruined shirt and spoke to the owner. Here's how the conversation went.

Me: "I'd like to show you something. Considering that you've laundered this shirt before, I have to assume that too much solution was used. What do you think happened?"

Owner (after inspecting the shirt for about thirty seconds): "The fabric is not good and the dye did not hold. I can't be held responsible for this."

Me: "But you've laundered this and three other identical shirts at least a half-dozen times. How is it that this flaw was only exposed now? What about the other shirts? They're made from the same fabric and they haven't been affected by this supposed defect."

Owner: "The dye did not hold. I did nothing wrong."

Me (slightly agitated): "Here's my ticket for clothing I'm picking up today. Let's take a look at the identical shirt, which you just laundered, and we can do a side-by-side comparison. Hopefully the shirt I'm picking up today didn't suffer the same fate."

Owner (after opening the newly laundered shirt and noticing no discoloring): "This is not the same shirt."

Me (beyond agitated): "Look at the labels! Both have identical labels; both have identical fabric blends, and when you put them side by side, you can clearly see that they are the same, identical shirt. The only differences are that one is blue and the other black, and now one is ready to wear and the other one is ruined. Please understand that I paid a lot of money for these shirts and I brought them to you in order to extend their lives. It's clear that there was some kind of mistake made which led to this shirt being damaged. What I'd like discuss is how—"

Know When To Break The First Rule

Owner (cutting me off midsentence): "Stop talking before I get angry. Nobody made a mistake, this fabric is no good."

Me (incredulous): "Before *you* get angry? I don't want to hear any more about the fabric. I brought this shirt to you for professional service and you failed. Are you going to make—" (and before I could finish asking, "Are you going to make good on this?")

Owner: "*No!*"

Me: "As you can see on the ticket, I am picking up quite a few items today. Am I to assume that you will be charging me for today's pickup?"

Owner: "*Yes!*"

And just like that, after twelve years, the relationship was over.

When we take a look at this exchange, it's quite clear where the dry cleaner failed: he immediately became defensive and continued, right to the end, to act defensively. And, as we all know, it's never a good idea to demand that your customer stop talking because it's making you angry. Aside from the obvious, what could the owner have done differently?

To begin, he should have immediately accepted responsibility in order to set the stage for an open dialogue. When a client walks in with a complaint, the first order of business is to ensure that the complaint is deemed valid (even when it isn't). Diffuse; do not deflect. Complaints are fantastic opportunities to strengthen client relationships by exceeding expectations. By creating an open dialogue, the owner could have explored several ways in which to further bond with an already loyal customer. The fact that he's providing a service also provides him with a low-cost opportunity to wow his customer. This could have occurred by offering "in-kind" service.

Let's take a look at a different version of this scenario: after examining the discolored shirt, the owner begins a dialogue.

Owner:	"Well, it looks like we might have done something wrong. Have you brought this shirt in to us for cleaning before?"
Me:	"Yes, I have. In fact, I have several of them, and they've all been cleaned here without incident. I'm picking one up from you today. Should we take a look and compare?"
Owner:	"It's not necessary. If this hasn't happened before, then I have to assume that in this instance there was some kind of bad reaction between the fabric and our solution. When did you buy this shirt, and how much did it cost?"
Me:	"I bought it, along with three others, last summer, and they each cost seventy-five dollars."

The owner now has at least two ways to wow me and keep me as a loyal customer. He can either suggest that the shirt has an expected lifespan of three years and divide the cost of the shirt by three and offer me a fifty-dollar credit, or he can take full responsibility for the entire seventy-five dollars. The fifty-dollar credit leaves me feeling good about doing business with this dry cleaner. The full seventy-five-dollar credit has me telling this story for weeks. Either way, he keeps a customer and it only costs him the price of the actual service, which is a fraction of the entire credit.

Here is what the owner could have said: "Mr. McConnell, you've been a long-standing, loyal customer. I know you've experienced a failure or two with us in the past, but it's clear that this shirt is beyond repair. I'm going to provide you with a full seventy-five-dollar credit, and we'll begin with today's bill of twenty dollars. I'll be sure to see that the remaining fifty-five dollars is applied to future service."

While I'm not in the dry-cleaning business, I'm comfortable in assuming the actual cost of this credit is probably about thirty-five dollars. Would you spend thirty-five dollars to keep a loyal customer?

Know When To Break The First Rule

I'm sure you would, but there's something else to consider—something more valuable than an immediate customer experience. By offering an in-kind credit, you are ensuring, maybe even guaranteeing, that your previously disappointed customer will return, which will provide you with an opportunity to continue to wow that customer with your own renewed sense of purpose. How much would you pay to provide that level of experience? More importantly, your customer will have a great story to tell. Perhaps the in-kind credit should be considered part of the marketing budget. In this instance, the owner assumed that I would continue to do business with him; he confused my loyalty with complacency.

The next scenario will also focus on a long-term client/vendor experience, but in this example, the vendor made an extremely unfortunate assumption by confusing my loyalty with gullibility. This assumption can be fatal to your business and your reputation. The following example will highlight a series of service failures, some of which may be occurring within your own organization.

I have lived in my current residence for more than twenty-three years, and during that time, I've utilized the same home heating-oil company. I have to admit that during that time, I'd grown complacent and continued to use their service because it was "good enough." I remained loyal in spite of now paying over $300 for a maintenance plan, which they used to provide at no charge. I've contemplated changing companies, but hadn't acted on it up to this point. Two weeks ago, I answered a knock on my door and was greeted by a young salesman from a competing oil company. He offered me a locked-in price of $2.79 per gallon, along with a service plan that was one-third the price than I was currently paying. Since I wasn't sure if $2.79 was a competitive price, I asked him if he would give me a few days to compare. Being a good salesperson, he drew up a contract and advised me that I had three days to make my decision. I then called my current provider and asked to speak with a pricing advisor; I was told someone would call back. Someone did call back—a day later. Here's how the conversation went:

Pricing Advisor (PA): "Before we begin, Mr. McConnell, I want to take this opportunity to thank you for being a loyal customer for more than twenty-three years. We appreciate your business and your loyalty. How can I assist you?"

Me: "Thank you for recognizing my loyalty. I'm sure you have preferred pricing for loyal clients, so tell me, what is your current 'locked-in' price?"

PA: "We have a very favorable price today. It is $3.58 per gallon."

Me: "$3.58? That's not acceptable."

PA: "Well, if you look at current pricing, you'll see that $3.58 is a very good price."

Me: "I'm looking at the current pricing on a contract from your competitor, and they're offering me $2.79 along with a service contract that's $200 less than yours."

PA: "Let me guess . . ." She then hissed the competitor's name through clenched teeth.

Me: "You really shouldn't disparage your competition; your tone is not acceptable. I'm asking you to provide me with a fair price. You thanked me for twenty-three years of loyalty and then insulted me with a price that is eighty cents per gallon more than your competitor. You should really be looking for ways to correct this situation, and you're not going to accomplish that by trying to diminish your competitor."

PA: "I can have you speak with a supervisor and they can explain our pricing policy to you."

Me: "No, I would prefer that you speak with your supervisors and explain the situation. It is up to you and your supervisors to keep me as a customer. Call me back by the end of the day and let me know what you can do."

I did receive a call later that day from the same pricing advisor. The price was now $2.99, and they could provide me with a lower-quality maintenance program for only $100. When I informed her that that still wasn't acceptable, she seemed flabbergasted and asked, "Well, what do you want?"

"What I want is to remain your customer. Talk to your supervisors and provide me with a solution that will keep me as a customer. Wow me. I'm not wowed with a price that remains twenty cents higher than your competitor's, and I don't want a lower-quality maintenance plan. I have one more day before I have to commit to your competitor's contract. Please get back to me with your best deal."

Well, I guess they couldn't come up with a better deal, because I never heard back from them. And just like with the dry cleaner, a long-term business relationship ended in a matter of moments. Unfortunately for them, these stories live on.

How does your company treat long-standing customers? Do you take them for granted, or do you reward them with pricing and service efficiencies? Always remember that your clients' perceptions are their realities, and their reality is your brand. The story they tell can either help to enhance or assist in destroying your brand.

Whenever I share this story, I am usually asked the same question: How could the pricing advisor recover from such a faux pas? After all, she began by thanking me for my patronage and then immediately insulted my loyalty by offering an obscenely high price. It's a fair question and I believe I have an answer. Once I told her that I had a contract that guaranteed me a much lower price, the pricing advisor could have quickly apologized and asked me to give her an opportunity to "make this right." Once I agreed (and most long-standing clients would), she should have then asked me to give her time to discuss the situation with her supervisors and then provided me with a specific time when she would call back. After that, it becomes incumbent upon that organization to make me feel special and appreciated; that can only be achieved by putting relationship ahead of profits.

In this case, the question the pricing advisor should have asked was: How do I keep this customer for another twenty-three years? Similar to the dry-cleaner scenario, she could have utilized in-kind service by providing a price lower than the competitor's and a free maintenance plan. If the competitor could afford $2.79 per gallon to woo me, then my long-term provider could certainly afford $2.69 to keep me. By not choosing this path, they succeeded in losing a long-standing customer.

When a customer shows loyalty, he or she is exhibiting trust. Trust is the best gift a client can bestow upon an organization. Long-term business relationships are, in most cases, free from competition. Your clients are assuming that you will put their best interests first. In the event that a long-standing customer feels taken advantage of, it is imperative that you restore his or her trust immediately. This is not the time to negotiate. Do everything in your power to wow that customer. Provide them with a credit for any perceived overcharge, lower their price, or provide an upgrade. Do anything you can to change their perception. In the following chapters, I discuss ways in which people buy, or don't buy, based on their emotional states, and you most definitely do not want to leave long-term clients feeling as if they have been taken advantage of. That is an emotional state that will have a resounding effect on your business and your reputation.

Know When To Break The First Rule

Take time over the next few days to make sure that you are recognizing your long-standing customers with loyalty of your own. Never confuse your customer's loyalty with gullibility. Loyalty equals trust. Live up to and exceed your clients' trust, along with their expectations.

Before I move on, it is important to note: should you go through the expense of purchasing a customer service management (CSM) software package and it provides pop-up windows that highlight important customer facts such as "years of service," make sure your customer service team does not use this information to simply acknowledge their patronage. Technology alone will never be a substitute for actually creating a superior customer experience. Never rely on technology to create a positive emotional state for your clients. Technology can provide you with information that can enhance a client relationship. When it comes to providing world-class service, think of technology as a behind-the-scene enhancement; it should be considered nothing more than an additional tool to use when delivering a positive customer experience.

It may, on the face of it, seem easy to separate yourself from the competition. These two examples only highlight the fact that so many companies and organizations are bereft of basic skills when it comes to client satisfaction. But I'm suggesting that you go beyond mere customer satisfaction and seek to deliver a total customer experience. Let me also suggest that's it not easy to create memorable customer experiences. In order to truly set your organization apart from the competition, you will have to create a culture of service and remain steadfast in your beliefs. Customer service is not a department; it's a culture. In this book, I will explain ways in which you can build this culture through the establishment of nonnegotiable standards. These standards will help your organization stand above the competition.

As a thirteen-year-old, I wasn't able to clearly articulate the connection between dry newspapers and bigger tips, but I did understand the strength of service. Years later, I was better able to appreciate how Bloomingdale's commitment to service enhanced the company brand. Before entering college, I was hardwired for service. I was able to recognize the opportunities to exceed a customer's expectations. These service skills led to a successful career in sales and, eventually, a successful business of my own. I was determined to always look through the lens of the client. This is a basic concept and a simple business philosophy, but it is not easy.

As you'll see in the following chapters, world-class customer service is not simply a smile and a handshake. World-class customer service is about culture. The right culture will drive the right behavior, which, in turn, will increase sales and strengthen customer loyalty. You will learn how to identify employees and recruits who possess the *service gene*, how to create nonnegotiable standards that will produce memorable customer experiences, how to retain your best employees through autonomy and empowerment and, most importantly, how to create a culture where clients *want* to do business with you.

This book is filled with real-life stories of people delivering unforgettable customer experiences. For these people, it's a way of life, not just a single event. Take these stories and use them to build your own culture of service. These stories should also help heighten your own awareness when you're either surprised or disappointed by a customer experience. You could be using your experiences in the creation of your own standards. Why was a specific customer experience great? Why was an experience only good, and what was needed to make it great? How could a bad experience have been avoided, and how could it have been used to exceed the customer's expectations?

Recently, I was talking with a friend and shared a particularly awful customer service story. I ended the story with the phrase "Can you believe this?" When I finished, there was silence for a few seconds before he said, "I don't know why you're surprised by bad customer service. I'm surprised whenever I receive *good* service."

Go out now and begin "surprising" your customers. Begin today and see if you don't notice a difference in yourself, your clients, your team, and your perception of the marketplace. Customer problems will suddenly become opportunities, and your competition will fade from your view as you begin to look through the lens of the customer. Suddenly, you'll see the business landscape become larger and more abundant. After all, there are so many customers just waiting to be surprised.

Chapter Two
CREATING A NONNEGOTIABLE SERVICE VISION

> You know I called my doctor on the telephone
> The lines were open, but there was nobody home
> Press one, press two, press pound, press three
> Why can't somebody just pick up the phone and talk to me?
> —Lyrics from "Keep it Simple," Keb' Mo'

We all suffer a strange paradox: we fight against change, yet we celebrate progress. We all know, but do not often acknowledge, that *progress is a result of change*. Ironically, change is the one constant in our lives. There are books written to help us prepare for change, such as *Who Moved My Cheese* by Spencer Johnson. There are motivational books and CDs available that celebrate and encourage change, like *Personal Power* by Tony Robbins. And yet, businesspeople tend to remain mired in their routines. We even make excuses to remain anchored to the status quo.

I'm often told, "Joe, we can talk about customer service all day; the fact remains that my product/service is a commodity. My clients buy price." When I hear this, I often suggest that they look through a different lens. Think about this for a moment. A commodity is a necessity, which means your clients and prospects *must* utilize your industry's product or service. Who they decide to use is a personal choice. Keep in mind that people don't buy products, services, or ideas. They buy emotional states. Think about your own buying habits. How many commodity purchases do you make where you bypass the lowest price in order to enjoy a buying experience? I utilize a specific dry cleaner not because they do a better job of cleaning my shirts, but because, even at a higher price, I enjoy a superior customer experience. I'm greeted by name, and at times, I'm offered an upgrade in service at no additional cost. Any problem is handled without argument and at no cost, and most importantly, I am thanked sincerely for my business. In short, I feel good when I walk out of that shop.

What are you doing to enhance your customer's emotional state? Do your clients consistently feel valued? If not, why not? Are you prepared to change your organization's philosophy and encourage a culture of service? Considering that you are reading this book, I have to assume the answer is *yes*. Let's begin by exploring ways in which you can make small, incremental adjustments within your organization that will yield immediate benefits for your customers.

ESTABLISH NONNEGOTIABLE SERVICE STANDARDS.

Nonnegotiable service standards must not to be confused with policy. Your employees should not be tethered to a policy manual. The goal is to always create memorable customer experiences. Every employee must lead in the mission to improve customer relationships, increase positive outcomes, and create memorable customer experiences. Nonnegotiable standards are built around an attitude of can do.

Your organization should be recognized and known for its can-do attitude, as in "we can do that." This sounds simple, and yet you will find it to be your most difficult challenge. It's imperative that all your employees never say no. They must learn that there are many ways of not saying yes without saying no. Customers don't want to be told no, or "we can't do that," even when the request does not play to your core competency. I'm not suggesting that you agree to a request that you cannot fulfill, but I am suggesting that your team should be prepared to provide an answer to any request that will leave your customer feeling special and important.

I was hired by a black-car service to present a series of customer service seminars. Despite a solid sales effort, the company's annual billings had not increased in more than three years. They were losing clients as fast as they were adding them. In order to prepare for the seminars, I sat in and observed their call center for two days. Everyone answering the phones was professional, well spoken, and efficient. Due to the high volume of calls, the representatives were overly concerned with the next call waiting in queue, and consequently, this resulted in most calls sounding rushed. The most glaring deficiency was the speed in which they hung up on clients who asked for service in locations where this company didn't operate. They had black cars available in New York City, New Jersey, and Connecticut.

I was amazed by the number of calls requesting service in major cities across the country. When I asked the owner about this, he explained that most of their clients were large banks, insurance companies, and law firms and that they had offices and clients in different cities. They were currently establishing strategic partnerships with car services in other cities but were still months away from rolling this out; contracts still needed to be signed, technology had to be upgraded, and the call center had to be trained. I suggested that they were missing opportunities to engage their clients and strengthen their relationships. He felt that his call center couldn't waste time on calls that weren't generating revenue. I asked him how much he spent on advertising and he told me more than half a million annually. They were spending half a million dollars on print ads and radio spots in an attempt to lure new business and strengthen their brand and then would hang up on their clients who needed a service that they did not provide. Does this sound familiar? Does your organization engage in this type of "efficient" behavior? Are you focusing only on immediate revenue while alienating some of your clients?

Imagine calling your trusted black-car service with an out-of-state request. Imagine this as a can't-do scenario, where you are told, "We don't provide service in that city. Is there anything else I can help you with? No? Good-bye." Now you're left with having to find another service. You will probably have to set up an account, fill out paperwork—well, you get the idea.

Now imagine this can-do scenario, where you are to tell your customer: "We don't currently provide service in that city, but we will be rolling out nationwide service in a few months. What I can do is have you speak with someone in senior management and they will take your information and book your reservation with one of our strategic partners. Give me just a moment and I will connect you with Mr. Powell."

The second scenario provided more than a solution for the client. It created a lasting impression on two levels. On the first level, the client's need was met. On the second level, it provided senior management with an opportunity to strengthen the relationship, both with the client and with the rest of the organization. When creating a culture of service by way of establishing nonnegotiable standards, it is important to understand that you are building a new top-down company culture. Everyone must be fully engaged when it comes to creating a memorable customer experience. Once you get the company culture right, superior customer service will follow.

This solution was created during one of our customer service workshops. Management volunteered to take these calls in order to free the call center from having to engage in a time-consuming process. It proved to be a wonderful opportunity for management to create a lasting customer experience. In addition, management learned more about their clients' buying habits, which, in turn, became this organization's marketing platform. The experience was so positive that even after deploying nationwide service, which could be quickly handled by the call center, management continued to take customer calls during peak hours as a way of separating themselves from the competition. These calls were not rushed. Management used this time to ask their clients about service and to thank them for their loyalty. In short, they separated themselves from the commodity marketplace by adding value. Focusing on opportunities to exceed customer expectations is the keystone in building nonnegotiable standards.

Let us take a look at what constitutes nonnegotiable standards. Your goal is to create a world-class service unique within your marketplace. When you achieve this, your organization will be viewed as a necessity rather than a commodity because your clients will *want* to do business with you.

The first step is to look at the similarities you share with your competition. Are there any real differences between your organization and your competition? If not, how can you create meaningful differences? In the case of the black-car service, its customers now feel as though they have a direct line to management. They now feel that their opinions and their business are important. You must create strengths that will elevate your business above the competition. The following examples can be applied to create immediate results:

- **Never say no.** We touched on this briefly with the example of the black-car service. It's important to understand just how negative *no* sounds when your client calls with a request. How many times have you bristled when you've been told no? In order to create a culture of service, your organization must maintain internal communication. This can be done by scheduling regular think-tank meetings to discuss client complaints and service weaknesses. Consistent complaints must be addressed and remedied. If an internal solution can't be created quickly, then an external solution needs to be put in place. How can you point your client toward a soft landing if you can't meet his or her request?

I recently used a travel agent to assist me in planning a fly-fishing trip to Ireland. The company did such a remarkable job that I called it again to help arrange a visit to Rome. Without hesitation, I was informed that they could book my visit, but they didn't possess the same level of vendor relationships in Italy as they did in Ireland and England. They then referred me to an agency that they knew could better meet my needs and provided me with a contact name and number. I have a seminar scheduled in London in a couple of months, and I'm sure you know who I'll be calling.

It is important to have answers at the ready, and the only way to do that is to anticipate client needs by maintaining an internal dialogue. Should you be unable to effectively meet your clients' needs, provide them with an option. L.L. Bean does this quite well. Whenever they are faced with an item on backorder, they offer to ship the item free of delivery charge once that item is restocked. Whether you decide to accept the later delivery is your decision, but you are left with the feeling that your business is important. Providing your team with solutions and empowering them to make decisions will make your clients feel less like a transaction and more like a valued customer.

- **Answer the phone.** This sounds like a basic business tenet, but I'm always amazed by the number of ways businesses discourage me from speaking to a representative. One of the most frustrating examples is automated answering systems complete with an IVR, or interactive voice response ("Say the last four numbers of your social security number"; "In order to better serve you," etc.). Equally frustrating is when you have a question and you go to a vendor website to look for a contact phone number and cannot find one. An organization will spend millions of dollars on ad campaigns, and yet it resists the opportunity to directly engage its clients and prospects.

The telephone is the best and cheapest of all branding devices available. Many companies may consider it out of fashion, but where else can you directly connect with your customer? Many organizations avoid opportunities to secure their clients' undivided attention for the sake of efficiency. Sounds illogical, doesn't it? Well, it is illogical and it is also bad business. Do you want to separate yourself from the commodity marketplace? Then—answer the phone! Zappos provides one of the best-known customer service experiences by talking with and engaging their customers. When you visit the Zappos website, the first thing you will notice is the company phone number, which is prominently posted on the home page. Take a look at a Lands' End catalog. At the bottom of each page, you'll find their phone number and website address, but the phone number is always listed first. These are organizations that want to speak with their customers.

As I mentioned earlier in this chapter, people buy emotional states. What emotional state are you in when you are forced to deal with an automated IVR or a website that is not accepting your order due to a forgotten password? Frustrated customers usually do not return, and they most definitely do not help sell your service or products to their business associates and friends. In order to create a memorable customer experience, it is necessary to create a positive emotional state, and this can only be accomplished through human contact. "People buy from people they like" is a well-known business adage. Create an environment where you answer the phone and connect with your customers. Your sales will increase when you create an emotional connection with your customers.

- **Everyone must be a creative problem solver.** It is important to limit processes and procedures when building a culture of service. When I was managing my own business, I insisted that my employees take responsibility and ownership for each transaction and any service defects. My service team had carte blanche when it came to client satisfaction. They provided the most sincere, yet creative, solutions or salves to a bruised client. Let's face it: we all fail our clients from time to time. It is inevitable. However, when your organization has built a culture of service around nonnegotiable standards, your clients will be more inclined to listen to a voice emitting a sense of ownership. In fact, they'll grow to expect nothing less. How your organization deals with defects will help define and brand your organization.

I recently read an account where a soldier, who was stationed in Iraq, ordered a pair of running shoes from Zappos (yes, the same company that "answers the phone"). When the shoes arrived, the soldier discovered that Zappos had sent the wrong size. He was a size eleven, but he had received a size ten. When he called Zappos, the representative noticed the APO address and asked if the caller was stationed in Iraq. When the soldier responded yes, he then advised him not to return the running shoes, but to give them to another soldier who wore a size ten. He was then told that a size eleven would be sent out that day and that Zappos would upgrade the delivery level at no additional charge. This was a creative solution that created a memorable experience for that soldier, which in turn found its way onto the Internet and into this book.

Are you using problems as opportunities to create memorable customer experiences? If you're not, then you are neglecting your customers and losing out on word-of-mouth advertising. Creative problem solving doesn't begin and end with the customer service department. Everyone within your organization must be sensitive to your client's needs. This can mean that your accounts billable department may have to customize invoicing to meet a client's request. Your IT department may have to integrate order processing with a client's internal system or build a program that provides unique reporting capabilities. Leave the one-size-fits-all mentality to your can't-do competitors. It's important that everyone within your organization recognizes the opportunities where he or she can provide a creative solution. You will find that by providing creative solutions for your clients, you will build lasting relationships.

- **Always sell the experience.** Everyone within your organization must always be focused on the customer's experience. You are not only selling a product or a service—you are, primarily, selling an experience. View your organization as a customer service company that just happens to be selling whatever it is you're providing (clothing, hamburgers, haircuts, etc.). Every transaction, large or small, should be treated as an opportunity to ensure your client's happiness. Some of you are familiar with Nordstrom's final touch to each purchase: after completing the transaction, the salesperson steps out from behind the counter, which removes any barrier between the customer and the merchant, in order to offer a face-to-face thank-you while at the same time handing the customer his or her new purchase. It is a small gesture of gratitude because the customer experiences appreciation.

Don't we all want to feel appreciated when we spend our money? Are there ways in which your organization can "step from behind the counter" after each transaction? Your organization will have to build a behind-the-scenes strategy designed to make your customers feel satisfied and appreciated in order to provide a positive experience. During a recent stay at the Four Seasons hotel in Santa Barbara, I was wowed when the valet brought out my car. The car had been washed and cleaned, and in my cup holder was a cold bottle of orange Gatorade. What made this special was the fact that when I first arrived at the hotel, I left an empty bottle of orange Gatorade in the cup holder. My expectations were already exceeded when the car arrived washed and cleaned, but when I slid into the driver's seat and discovered a cold bottle of my favorite soft drink, I experienced a sense of caring: someone was paying attention—to me!

Once again, this was a small gesture that cost very little and yielded huge benefits. Whenever someone tells me that they are planning to visit Santa Barbara, I strongly urge them to stay at the Four Seasons. Are you creating the type of experiences that would compel your customers to strongly urge their associates and colleagues to purchase your product or service? Nonnegotiable customer experiences must be established in order to create word-of-mouth sales and client loyalty. We know from our own buying experiences that a single memorable experience can override disappointment. Last year, I had dinner at Ben Benson's Steak House in New York City. At first, my friend and I were seated at a small, cramped table next to the front door. When I asked for a different table, the maitre d' seemed put out. Upon being seated at a larger, less cramped table, the waiter brought out a bread basket, and I was disappointed again when I found a half-eaten roll. Within the first ten minutes, I was given a bad table, treated condescendingly by the maitre d', and repulsed by a "used" dinner roll.

My friend and I were about to get up and leave when our waiter approached to take our drink orders. I recounted the recent events and told the waiter that we were not staying for dinner. He asked us to reconsider and suggested that he would personally see to it that we would have a memorable meal. "If you'll allow me, let's start all over. Just give me a chance to change your mind about Ben Benson's," he said. How could I refuse that offer? He began by whisking the offending bread basket off the table and returned with a fresh selection of bread along with our cocktails, which were on the house. Dessert was gratis too. The dinner and service was fantastic, and I returned the following day to speak with Ben Benson himself. I felt compelled to let Ben know how his waiter was able to turn a bad situation into a memorable dinner. Needless to say, along with my favorite hotel in Santa Barbara, I often recommend my favorite steak house in New York City. Ben Benson's established nonnegotiable experiential standards, and yet, I experienced three cracks in the system. No matter how hard we work to ensure an airtight service environment, there will be times when the system and our people fail. That is why it's imperative to maintain your culture of service every day; you and your team must stay on the message. At Ben Benson's, the culture ran deep enough and wide enough to catch and repair any defects.

I began this chapter by discussing the paradox of change. We fight change, but we celebrate progress. The creation of nonnegotiable service standards represents profound change. There is no other option; everyone on your team must abide by the standards you put in place. You can only establish a culture of service by building an airtight service environment. During my seminars I am almost always told, "We're too busy to adhere to these standards. Isn't it unrealistic to suggest that we live up to these standards every day?" I admit that it is hard work to build a culture of service. But what is the alternative? To remain mired in the ordinary? To settle for mediocrity? To remain a commodity? I challenge you to take the initiative and drive progress by creating a culture that will make your organization extraordinary. There will be people within your organization who will push against this new culture; they will find reasons why it is unrealistically utopian and operationally inefficient.

The message must begin at the top and it must be reinforced every day. The results will be magical. Your clients will become more loyal, and through word-of-mouth advertising, they will become your best sales generator. Your customers will be happy, your business will grow, and your employees will feed off the positive energy of a job well done. Additionally, you will attract competent people who will want to work at your organization. The next chapter will deal with attracting, screening, hiring, and retaining good people. These changes are going to require personalities who understand the culture of service. The biggest challenge will be getting your front-line employees, who are usually the lowest paid, to adhere to your organization's nonnegotiable standards. That is why it is important to have the right people in place, because the right people will do the right thing at the right time—every time. By resisting change, you resist progress.

Chapter Three
ESTABLISHING NONNEGOTIABLE HIRING STANDARDS

We already discussed the value of creating nonnegotiable customer experiences. The next step is identifying the people who can assist you in achieving that goal. Let me begin by stating that good customer service people are born with the service gene. People who understand the power of exceeding clients' expectations are hardwired with unique skills. I will dissect those skills later in this chapter. Before I continue, I want to share an expression that I've heard many times from a business owner who was notorious for making bad hiring decisions. Whenever he terminated an employee, he said the following: "You never know who you hire, just who you fire." What an absurd concept. His inability to properly evaluate his prospects was his problem, not the person whom he hired. The goal is to ensure that the people you hire possess all the necessary traits to succeed in your organization. This can only be achieved by establishing nonnegotiable hiring standards. It is your responsibility to enhance your team and your service vision by hiring the right people. Do not hire the resume. Hire the personality.

A coach cannot teach athletes to run fast. They can be taught skills that help them run faster, but if they aren't born with an overabundance of quick-twitch muscles, they aren't going to be able to run fast no matter how hard they are coached. The same is true in other areas as well, such as music and art. We've all experienced that moment when we discovered that we didn't possess the talent necessary to become a professional baseball player or a member of the London Philharmonic. Everyone is talented at something, and when we discover our dominant skills, we work hard to achieve our goals. Just as a professional basketball team won't accept a player without superior basketball skills, you shouldn't accept anyone on your team who doesn't possess superior service skills. In this chapter, we'll look at ways in which you can identify the right people who will adhere to, and improve upon, your company's service vision.

Let us begin by looking at the people already on your team. Ask yourself honestly: How many truly possess the service gene? This will be a difficult exercise because, once again, you are faced with the prospect of having to make changes. Begin first with your front-line employees. These are the employees who most often touch your customers. Are they always looking through the lens of the customer, or are they looking through the lens of least effort? Which members of your team are most often concerned about the client's needs and expectations? In order to highlight the importance of front-line employees, let's look at an example where they can either make or break a customer experience.

How many times have you walked into a store to either ask a question or make a purchase only to be ignored while two sales clerks carried on a personal conversation? When walking into a retail shop, we expect prompt and courteous service. However, there are times when we are met with rudeness and incompetence. How can this happen? Perhaps the better question is, why does this happen? It happens because either the department manager or the store manager does not monitor and control the hiring standards. This is further exasperated by not reinforcing the required service standards. Even worse is when the managers actually encourage bad behavior because they are not motivated to focus on a culture of service. In short, everyone's going through the motions. Have you ever walked into a store where, in spite of a cloud of bad service, a salesperson emerges who clearly enjoys his job and remains steadfast in creating an unforgettable customer experience? That salesperson

Know When To Break The First Rule

possesses the inherent skills necessary to create unforgettable customer experiences—the same skills and determination that you should look for when you put your team in place. In fact, I am suggesting that the next time you experience an above-and-beyond service moment and it is a result of one person's determined effort, give that person your business card and ask that person to come in for an interview! You should always be looking for people whom you want on your team.

I often make that suggestion to my clients, but they argue that the salesclerk, while in possession of an above-and-beyond service gene, doesn't know the first thing about their business. My answer is this: the first and last thing about business can be taught, but service aptitude is a God-given talent. The next time you enjoy a memorable customer experience, whether it be at a store, restaurant, airport, or local car wash, watch closely how the customer service person interacts with you. Usually, you will witness strong eye contact, positive language, good questions and listening skills and, most importantly, a desire to be helpful. People with the right service aptitude take every customer experience, both good and bad, personally. Don't you want people who take ownership of each transaction and challenge themselves and their coworkers to exceed customer expectations? Once again, I suggest to you that such people are in possession of a unique set of skills, and you should not settle for anything less than world-class talent. In order to create a team of superstars, you will be required to create nonnegotiable hiring standards. These standards will be built around the hardwired traits inherent in all world-class service leaders.

At the beginning of the chapter, I mentioned evaluating your current employees. As you read through these nonnegotiable standards, the first thing you must do is hold your current team up to these standards. Imagine, if you will, that you are interviewing your current team. You will have to ask yourself difficult questions, and you may be forced to make difficult decisions. Always remember: change is difficult, but change is *progress*.

Early in the interview process, it is imperative that you determine whether or not the candidates possess the basic traits of a hardwired service leader. They must be organized, attentive, well groomed, polite, well spoken, positive, passionate, and compassionate. Most importantly, each candidate must be empathetic to your organization's service vision and sensitive to your client's expectations. If any of these traits are absent, you'd be well advised to move on to another candidate. In addition, you should be prepared to invest time in the interview process. This important step cannot be rushed. I often suggest that the interview process include focused interviews that include several applicable department heads and at least one lunch or dinner. Sharing a meal is essential because you will learn about that candidate's service foundation. Does the candidate speak down to the wait staff? How are his or her table manners? Does the candidate come across as appreciative or entitled? It will be well worth your while to observe your candidates in a social setting where they are viewed as the customers. How they act as a customer will speak to how they will act or react to your customers.

Take time to handpick the best candidates, and take the time to ensure that they buy into your organization's service vision both through word and action. Always remember, you are adhering to nonnegotiable hiring standards. Once you've determined that they possess the basic traits listed above, you will then need to confirm that they possess more-advanced customer-centric skills, such as the following:

- **Enthusiasm.** Without enthusiasm, it is impossible to be creative and passionate. In order to create a culture of service, you must surround yourself with people who possess the positive energy that can only be built on a foundation of enthusiasm. Your

Know When To Break The First Rule

clients need to feel the excitement each time they call or visit. People buy emotions, and genuine enthusiasm will always bring about a positive response. This is not to suggest that your service team should sound like cheerleaders or motivational speakers. Your clients should feel as though their call is welcomed and their business appreciated.

During the interview process, you must be confident that the candidate's enthusiasm is genuine and honest. There is a level of confidence that emanates from someone in possession of honest enthusiasm. These candidates are confident, not only of their skills, but also of their worth. You cannot rattle or faze them during the interview. They will always remain positive and in control, even if they don't have an answer to a difficult interview question. Isn't that what you want your customers to sense every time they call? It is impossible to possess all the other nonnegotiable service skills without enthusiasm. With enthusiasm comes the important can-do attitude, which is essential when building a culture of service, and this is why enthusiasm is the single most important trait in building a customer-focused team.

We all know people who, no matter the circumstance, always remain positive and enthusiastic. During the course of your life, haven't you found yourself drawn to these people? Don't you find their energy magnetic? On a friend's recommendation, I recently visited Durso's, an Italian specialty food shop, in Queens, New York. I had never been to Durso's before, but upon walking in, I was immediately taken by the huge selection of Italian delights. When I approached the counter, I was greeted by a young man with a big smile and a willing attitude. When I placed my order, the young clerk asked what I was using the prosciutto for. I told him it was for a brussels-sprout recipe and all I knew was that it included butter and prosciutto. He immediately became animated and excited. He had never before heard of these ingredients being used in a brussels-sprout dish and asked if I would be kind enough to provide him with the recipe. He then handed me his business card, which included his e-mail address. He then asked me to follow him down to the end of the counter, where he was able to come out from behind the counter and hand me my purchase (similar to Nordstrom's). He thanked me for shopping at Durso's and asked to please remember to send him the recipe. He was sincerely enthused about food, recipes, and service.

Since the recipe required just a few slices of prosciutto, my bill came to $3.75. I received all that attention and personal connection for a $3.75 purchase. Only someone sincerely enthusiastic could have created such a memorable customer experience. For the record, I did provide this young man with the recipe. However, instead of using e-mail, I went back to Durso's to hand-deliver the recipe and to purchase homemade ravioli, sausage, and imported tomatoes, and this time my bill was much more than $3.75. Despite Durso's being more than ten miles from my home, I continue to visit their shop whenever I'm in need of fine Italian ingredients. On a side note, during my last visit, I saw the same brussels-sprout dish in their prepared food section.

It is important to note that this young clerk possessed all of the nonnegotiable traits needed to create a memorable customer experience, but what truly captured my attention was his enthusiastic attitude. I was compelled to provide him with the recipe because his excitement was sincere and contagious. He succeeded in making an emotional connection that created a lasting impression. Do the members of your team possess this level of enthusiasm? It will become apparent as you explore the following nonnegotiable service skills how important and essential it is to be enthusiastic. Not every client experience will be positive—some will be complicated and difficult—but enthusiasm can assist in propelling even the most negative experience into a positive and lasting impression. Do not underestimate the power of enthusiasm.

- **The ability to embrace problems.** People in possession of the service gene understand the value within a service defect; they use problems as a way to enhance the client relationship. Think about this for a moment: almost every memorable customer service story begins with a disappointment, sometimes a profound disappointment. In the previous chapter, I told the story of the half-eaten dinner roll (yuck!) at Ben Benson's Steak House. The waiter used my disappointment as a springboard to exceed my expectations and create a memorable customer experience.

In another example, the day before his son's wedding, a friend of mine, Bob, picked up his new suit, which he bought and had tailored at Saks Fifth Avenue. Upon trying it on, he discovered that both pant legs were tailored two inches too short. There wasn't even enough fabric left to correct the mistake. The salesperson assisted Bob in choosing another, more expensive suit, had his best tailor handle the fitting, and had the suit hand-delivered to Bob's home the next morning in time for the wedding and at no additional cost. In the breast pocket was a thank-you card offering congratulations along with a one-hundred-dollar gift certificate. Bob never would have told me that story if not for the service defect. I heard that story repeated no less than five times, each time by a different person during the course of the reception.

That is the power created by word-of-mouth advertising, and word-of-mouth advertising is created by memorable customer experiences. When identifying a potential team member, you must ascertain whether or not that person understands the importance of embracing and taking ownership of a problem. When a client calls to complain, they are usually saying, "I like your company, but I have a problem." This is the sweet spot for any proactive customer service rep, and it should be the sweet spot for all your employees. As you continue to build your organization's culture of service, complaints should be viewed as opportunities to wow the customer. The ability to embrace problems and to view them as opportunities is a nonnegotiable standard when hiring and retaining employees.

Many competent service professionals are well skilled at providing world-class service, but most have not acquired the mastery of reading a client's disappointment and recognizing the inherent golden opportunity. Most, in fact, run from or deflect the problem to another person or department. Let's take another look at my friend Bob's wedding-suit story. Suppose the salesperson had looked to put the blame on the tailoring department (where it belonged); then the tailor would have to explain himself and apologize. A manager would then be summoned and he would also offer an apology. The salesperson would get defensive and suggest that the tailor fix the problem, and Bob would be standing there wondering what he was going to wear to his son's wedding.

Many service professionals would side with the salesperson. "He did his job. He sold a suit and the tailor screwed up the job. Let the tailor fix it." Instead, the salesperson took ownership and control, and any issue he would have had with the tailor could have been handled behind the scenes and remained invisible to Bob. The salesperson succeeded in creating a memorable customer experience without embarrassing the tailoring department (which likely enhanced morale) and established a lifelong customer, complete with word-of-mouth advertising. This inherent skill-set is essential. You must be completely convinced that your new-hire is acutely aware of the opportunities where he or she can exceed customer expectations.

- **The ability to look through the lens of the customer.** We are all familiar with the phrase "walk in another man's shoes." While we understand its implications, very few of us live by that credo. The general attitude in the current business environment is one of "what's in it for me?" When someone goes out of his way to ensure our satisfaction, we are surprised, sometimes even shocked. The surprise ingredient is what gives this trait its wow factor. This can be something as easy as providing an upgrade. How pleased are you when, upon check-in at a hotel, the desk clerk bumps you up to a suite? How about an upgrade to business class on an airline? Now that's a wow!

This can be often accomplished just by asking a question; something as simple as a concierge asking, "How did your business meeting go today, Mr. Jones?" A door can be opened to a lasting business relationship simply by using a customer's name and asking an appropriate question. Your front-line employees must be skilled in this area. They need to be able to read their customers and provide a personal connection and a solution to a need or problem. This skill is inherent in the service gene, and not everyone possesses this ability.

When I was running my own business, the customer service team took it upon themselves to create efficiencies for their clients. I was the owner of a transportation/logistics company, and our clients had high-volume days each week in addition to seasonal spikes. Once the service team identified the high-volume patterns, they built custom reports and volume matrixes to help streamline the processes during these high-volume spikes. These tools proved to be valuable timesavers for the clients. Additionally, the day before a predicted volume spike, the assigned service rep would call each of his or her clients with answers before the questions were asked. The questions were easily predicted (truck schedules, estimated deliver times, etc.), but no other competing service was providing this kind of efficiency. As a result, we built an airtight service environment, which protected us from competition and resulted in additional growth.

Most importantly, I did not have to prompt this type of action. All I did was encourage an atmosphere of service. As a result, a healthy competitive environment emerged. Each service rep was looking for ways to out-do his or her colleagues and the results were outstanding. During my time of ownership, my organization enjoyed a 100 percent client retention rate. This can only be achieved in a high-energy, self-managed environment. Everyone within your organization should be looking through the lens of the customer and identifying ways in which he or she can exceed expectations and create a lasting impression.

You may find that you have additional nonnegotiable hiring standards unique to your business or industry as you enter into the recruitment phase. Please remain steadfast in your nonnegotiable mindset when you include these standards to your recruitment policy. There are three questions directly connected to the nonnegotiable hiring standards that you should be asking yourself during the interview process:

1. Can this recruit get to know more about my customer than my competitor?
2. Can this recruit get closer to my customer than my competitor?
3. Can this recruit emotionally connect with my customer?

The goal is to have all your clients thinking and saying, "I love doing business with these guys. They take the stress out of doing business and make my life easier."

Having assisted many organizations in building and enhancing their customer service vision, I've noticed an unusual trend: many of the best hires come from either outside the industry or outside a direct customer service department. For example, a few years ago, I was asked to serve as a hiring advisor to a high-end, custom-kitchen showroom. Their salespeople were knowledgeable and professional, but their sales remained flat and the owners noticed that they weren't receiving as many word-of-mouth referrals as they had hoped. It is important to note that the salespeople remained as the point of contact beginning with the sale and ending with final installation. Consequently, they were both salespeople and customer-service reps. This is a great concept when you have the right people. In this example, we decided to step outside the industry and look for recruits who weren't familiar with traditional showroom sales, although we believed that industry knowledge would be helpful. We didn't have to search too far.

I began this chapter by suggesting that you should always be looking for people who possess the service gene. In this instance, we had just completed several hours of first-round interviews and found ourselves underwhelmed by the initial crop of candidates. The owners and I were walking through the showroom when we noticed a man wearing work clothes and talking with one of the showroom sales reps. He was there with a young couple, and they were looking for new cabinets and countertops for their soon-to-be newly renovated kitchen. It became apparent that this man was their contractor, and he was offering advice regarding space and function. We immediately noticed that he was fully engaged and enthused, and he was making sure that his clients' best interests were being served. In all fairness, the showroom rep was knowledgeable and engaging, but he was being outsold by the contractor. The man in carpenter pants and flannel shirt was the authority. He understood every concept connected to installation, practicality, and durability ("I wouldn't put that cabinet with that type of finish over a stove; over time, the heat will lead to discoloration."). Even more pronounced was his body language. He put his clients and the sales rep at ease with his calm confidence, broad smile, easy laugh, and direct eye contact. I suggested to the owners that we approach him and schedule an interview.

Know When To Break The First Rule

This was a profound paradigm shift for the owners. They were accustomed to a younger, more polished-looking, eloquent-speaking sales rep. After all, they were selling kitchen renovations in excess of $100,000. I suggested that we schedule an interview if for no other reason than as a learning exercise. The contractor, whose name was Larry, was in the process of selling his general-contractor business, but at sixty years old, he felt he was too young to retire. He told us during the first interview, "The best part of my job is providing my clients with a finished product that exceeds their original vision. Nothing is more satisfying than seeing my clients overjoyed with their new living space."

He explained to us that he was weary from dealing with subcontractors who didn't meet his "admittedly high expectations," and was disappointed by the "eroding standards within the industry." As a result, he found himself having to "anticipate service failures" and spent much of his time "heading them off." He was an amateur chef, and his favorite project was installing new kitchens. Let us take a closer look at this first interview before moving on to the subsequent interviews. While Larry wasn't intrinsically a customer-relations salesperson, he did possess the necessary first-round qualities: he was organized, attentive, well groomed (he wore a suit to the interview), polite, well spoken, positive, passionate, and compassionate. Additionally, he displayed all three of our nonnegotiable hiring standards:

- **enthusiasm**—Nothing satisfied him more than an overwhelmed customer and, of course, there was his passion for cooking.
- **the ability to embrace problems**—He possessed the advanced ability to anticipate problems and head them off. He was embracing problems before they occurred.
- **the ability to look through the lens of the customer**—We had witnessed that quality a few days prior in the showroom.

He fully understood his client's expectations and played the role of trusted advisor.

Most importantly, he possessed his own nonnegotiable standards when it came to service and client satisfaction. Take a look at the words and phrases he used:

- "my own, admittedly high, expectations"
- "a finished product that exceeds [his client's] original vision"
- "seeing my clients overjoyed with their new living space"
- "disappointed by the eroding standards within the industry"

We decided to break the second interview into two phases. The first phase consisted of a series of what-ifs. What if a delivery is late and the contractor already has an installation team in place? What if a client insists on a product or design that you know will lead to disappointment? What if a contractor comes into the showroom with clients and begins to feel threatened by your advanced knowledge? What if a client complains about one of our suggested contractors? The owners had prepared a series of questions, and we watched and listened carefully as Larry worked his way down this list with the calm confidence of a person who had experienced most of the what-ifs in life. His enthusiasm was evident by his confident demeanor. I almost expected him to ask, "Is that all you got?"

The second phase consisted of having Larry meet and spend time with a few of the current sales reps. This can become sticky, because current employees might feel threatened by a perceived intruder. The owners and I left the showroom for a couple of hours, which gave Larry an opportunity to determine, without our involvement, whether this career move would be advantageous for him. I was certain that this was the right move for Larry, but I was concerned that the current showroom reps would react with hostility and fear, thereby making this an untenable option. When we returned, the energy in the showroom was high and positive. Larry was assisting one of the reps, who was working with a client. One of the newer reps approached the owners and expressed enthusiasm at the idea of having Larry aboard as an "invaluable resource and advisor." Larry's nonthreatening demeanor, born of confidence and experience, had won over what I expected to be the most difficult hurdle. At this point, I don't think any of us was surprised.

I'm sure I don't have to tell you that our dinner interview was superfluous, but it did provide us with a remarkable moment. Larry's enthusiasm around food was contagious. He explained the various techniques employed in preparing our meals and he did so with the enthusiasm of a person filled with passion and love for food. Now here's what made this a remarkable moment, especially when it came to creating a superior customer experience: unbeknownst to us our waiter overheard our conversation and informed the chef that there was a table of, as he put it, "enthused and knowledgeable foodies." When the chef came out to take our dessert order and to thank us for our business, we were pleasantly surprised. When he returned and joined us for dessert, which he had personally prepared, we were stunned. When he discovered that everyone at the table was in the custom-kitchen business, he became even more animated, and our dessert course carried on for almost two hours. Larry's enthusiasm was indeed contagious, and our waiter assisted in creating a lasting impression.

I'm pleased to report that Larry took the job and has been very successful. The upshot is that his knowledge, insight, and enthusiasm rippled through the showroom; many of the showroom reps utilize Larry for advice and guidance. Word-of-mouth sales went from barely ten percent to almost fifty percent. As a result, the advertising budget has been cut by two-thirds. Oh, and one more thing: I've been back to that restaurant at least a dozen times.

In closing this chapter, I want to stress, once again, the importance of setting clearly defined, nonnegotiable hiring standards. In the example I just used, Larry represented change. For the owners, it was a profound change, and for the existing employees, it could have been a threatening change. While Larry didn't truly represent a change from outside the industry, he did represent a change in hiring protocol. We first observed him wearing jeans, work boots, and a flannel shirt. Pay attention to the talented, service-oriented people you encounter every day and ask, "Will this person fit into my service vision? Does this person possess the service gene?" If the answer to both these questions is yes, take a chance and give that person your business card and schedule an interview.

Not every candidate will meet your criteria. You have to take chances in order to build a sustaining culture of service. Scheduling interviews with potential service professionals will probably be the least risky of all the chances you take in your business endeavors. Be certain to adhere to your nonnegotiable standards and you'll reduce your risk. Be sure to rethink your past hiring practices. What are you achieving by hiring within your industry? You could be hiring candidates with preconceived notions and industry-related bad habits. You have to ask yourself, If they're any good, why are they available? Why would their current employer let them leave?

Good ideas often come from outside your industry. Good people do also, and they bring no preconceived notions or baggage. When establishing your nonnegotiable hiring standards, there is only one steadfast rule: everyone should be focused on creating memorable customer experiences—all day, every day!

Know When To Break The First Rule

When I assist clients in building an interview format, I usually begin by asking them to identify their most customer-centric employees. Then I ask them to list all their best traits. I break this list into two categories. The first category is labeled *competency*, and the second is labeled *characteristics*. Competency traits would include: computer literate, well organized, and strong managerial skills. Character traits include: friendly, courteous, thorough, positive, enthusiastic, team player, problem solver, and empathetic. There will always be a larger number of character traits than competency traits when describing a customer-focused personality. Competencies can be learned. Customer-centric character traits cannot be taught. A basic rule when hiring customer-focused employees is this: when you hire a person, you are hiring his or her *judgment*. That is to say that you are hiring someone for his ability to make judgments regarding customer satisfaction. When you approach the interview process from this direction, you will find yourself in a more confident position. You will only hire the right people because you will be hiring traits, not resumes. No smart business leader has ever hired a resume. If you were hiring a surgeon, you would choose skill over bedside manner, but you are not hiring surgeons; you are building a highly motivated team made up of customer-centric personalities. Make sure you hire people with the right skills.

In the next chapter, I will focus on incenting, motivating, and retaining all the quality people you have on your team. Business is about ownership, and we'll discuss different ways your organization can create a sense of ownership. Ownership equates with a "buy-in" philosophy, which, in turn, equates with loyalty—which equals continuity and leads to client loyalty and turbo-charged revenue and profits. Every businessperson knows it's more expensive to gain new business than it is to retain existing business. Similarly, it's more expensive to recruit quality employees than it is to retain experienced, high-performing employees.

Chapter Four
RE-RECRUITING YOUR BEST EMPLOYEES THROUGH OWNERSHIP AND EMPOWERMENT

In the previous chapter, I discussed the importance of identifying and recruiting people in possession of the service gene. This search should always be ongoing. You should be relentless when it comes to securing and adding quality employees to your organization. Another question you should be asking is: How do I retain my best employees? If you follow the steps described in the previous chapter, you will know just how labor-intensive and time-consuming this process can be. It is one thing to be on the lookout for new team members; it is another thing to have to replace a valued employee. You must always be prepared to lose quality people. Some employees will move to another state, go back to school, or leave to start a family, but you never want to lose an important teammate due to neglect or complacency. In this chapter, we'll discuss ways in which you can reduce turnover and, at the same time, motivate your team by creating an atmosphere of healthy competition. Earlier, I described how your customers buy emotional states. In this chapter, we'll look at ways in which you can create positive emotional states for your team. Comradeship, ownership, autonomy, and authority are the ingredients for creating positive emotional states within your organization. Think back on your own career and I'm sure you'll link a negative emotional state to jobs where you were reduced to navigating through layers of management and procedures. Conversely, if you were fortunate enough to have worked for an organization where systems were streamlined and customer satisfaction was put ahead of policy, you can appreciate the excitement and sense of accomplishment that comes from meeting and exceeding customer expectations.

If you've remained steadfast in your nonnegotiable hiring standards, you should have a dynamic, self-motivating team in place. Now it's up to you to assist in maintaining that high-energy vibe. Still, even the most enthusiastic personalities can fall into a pothole of inertia and complacency. Affirmations and recognition will provide some short-term motivation, but the real challenge will come in finding a consistent motivator. The motivator is money for many organizations, and I agree that money is what gets all of us up in the morning and into the daily rigors of life. Nevertheless, you have committed yourself to establishing an energized atmosphere built on the daily creation of memorable customer experiences, and within that highly charged atmosphere, there is no room for complacency. Let us take a look at how, through empowerment and ownership, you can re-recruit your team every day.

I concluded the previous chapter by suggesting that ownership builds morale and, in turn, market share. Ownership comes in many different packages; for most businesspeople, it represents company shares, profit sharing, bonus plans, or partnerships. I am going to move away from revenue-related definitions for this part of the chapter and focus, initially, on the altruistic definition of ownership. I have to assume that you have assembled a team of enthusiastic, self-motivated people and in doing so you are paying them better than a mere, life-sustaining wage; otherwise, why would they have moved over to your organization? Later in this chapter, we'll discuss ways in which you can turbo-charge productivity through bonuses and profit sharing, but first, let's look at ways in which client ownership can build morale, drive sales, and create a positive emotional state for everyone on your team.

This process should be quite easy assuming that you have the right team in place. In fact, you should think of yourself as a minimalist; you have the right people in the right culture, which should result in minimal management. It's important to remember that your culture of service is built around the steady creation of unforgettable client experiences. If you have conveyed this philosophy effectively, you should now have an environment where all your teammates are working together to separate your organization from the competition. When you are working with people in possession of the service gene, you would be ill-advised in trying to micromanage them. Instead, be diligent in setting the goal, and then let your team set about in wowing your clients. When you give your employees autonomy and the freedom to make decisions based on client satisfaction, you will discover that traditional forms of management will only hold them back from achieving your vision. Trust and confidence will become the centerpiece of your organizational platform. Be confident that everyone in your organization understands that client satisfaction is of primary importance, and be equally confident that increased sales and profits will soon follow.

Take a moment to think about a few of your more memorable customer experiences, and be sure to look at both positive and negative experiences. I have to believe that most, if not all of those experiences, involved a one-on-one relationship where you were either purchasing a product or were working through a product or service defect. Why were those experiences memorable? If the experience was positive, I'm confident in assuming that it was because the process was efficient and that the representative you were working with was sure that your experience was fulfilling from start to finish. Likewise, if the experience was negative, it was probably because your one-on-one relationship decayed and you found yourself waiting for a manager or supervisor to assist in the process. Are you more impressed when your purchase or complaint is handled quickly and efficiently with as little outside intervention as possible? Do you find yourself wowed when a representative takes you through a purchase or resolution with enthusiasm and a sense of ownership?

I am always impressed when I'm calling with a problem and I hear the following, "I'm sorry you were disappointed, Mr. McConnell. I'm here to ensure your satisfaction; now, please, tell me what happened." However, if that same representative, after hearing my story, informs me that they now have to transfer me to a supervisor, my impression will immediately sour and I'll no longer be wowed. In an earlier chapter, I used my experience at Ben Benson's Steak House to highlight a positive customer experience. The waiter took it upon himself to change my mind about Ben Benson's after I suffered a series of service defects. What made that experience memorable was his sense of ownership. Once he took ownership of that problem, he made sure no one else was involved. He didn't ask for permission to buy us our drinks or to provide us with desserts on the house. Clearly, the waitstaff at Ben Benson's are tasked only with client satisfaction, and they do it with a sense of duty and ownership. True service leaders do not want to work within the confines of procedures and policy. Good customer service isn't a result of policy and procedure. It's a result of excellent behavior. By tasking your team with client ownership, you are stripping away the layers of management that result in delayed decision making and, inevitably, inertia. If your organization isn't taking action, then your clients will. They will defect and go in search of an organization that will recognize their needs and act on them with a sense of urgency.

Most dynamic business plans begin with a vision of the finished product. In this case, you should be starting with the client's experience and then begin looking at the entire end-to-end experience. How will you ensure consistently memorable customer experiences? You have the team in place, you are staying on message when it comes to your culture of service, and every day, you are identifying people in possession of the service gene. You've created an above-and-beyond culture both for yourself and your organization. Now it's time to empower your team and provide them with the authority to make decisions advantageous to their clients and your organization. This sense of ownership becomes a tool for success. The most driven, responsible, service-oriented people are frustrated by an inability to exact satisfaction. When you hire a person with service aptitude, you are hiring a can-do personality with impatience for delay or inaction. These are highly charged people with a sense of mission. Imagine an organization where the service gene is mandatory, yet everyone is required to work within procedural parameters. I'm frustrated just by writing that sentence. It is similar to imagining a field of highly charged, muscle-twitching thoroughbreds straining at starting gates that will never open. It's up to you to dispense with the starting gate.

There are a lot of things you will have to do in order to build a culture of service. It won't be easy. It will require determination and a steadfast belief in power of customer satisfaction. When making a concerted decision to separate yourself from the commodity marketplace, you will be faced with a new set of decisions. This will require that you abandon your current management style and adapt a flat organizational structure. I will suggest at this juncture that the most important decisions you make are not the things you do, but rather, the things you decide *not* to do. The first thing you should decide *not* to do is handcuff your service team with policy. Instead, enhance your charged environment with celebration. Be sure to celebrate both success and failure. People hardwired with the service gene embrace ownership and begin to look for creative ways to wow the customer. Sometimes creativity will push conventional barriers. It will be up to you to *not* repress creative impulses.

Know When To Break The First Rule

Let's take a look at a memorable customer experience that I described in an earlier chapter. I described an experience where a valet returned my car with a bottle of chilled Gatorade in my cup holder. Let us hypothesize for a moment and assume that this wasn't hotel policy and the valet took it upon himself to replace the empty container with a fresh bottle of Gatorade. Policy notwithstanding, I was impressed enough to tell this story and to recommend the same hotel for years afterward. Would it have made sense for the manager to question the valet, possibly challenging the valet as to whose budget the seventy-nine-cent Gatorade should be charged? Suppose it wasn't policy and the manager noticed and celebrated the initiative during the next valet meeting and insisted that it become policy. Perhaps the manager went so far as to set up a separate budget and refrigeration unit to house a variety of popular soft drinks and bottled water just for this use. Imagine the positive energy built around this initiative. The valet feels validated and everyone is encouraged to take the initiative when it comes to creating memorable customer experiences. The effects are two-fold: this becomes a highly charged, exciting workplace where clients enjoy world-class service, and both the employees and customers are wowed. Positive energy creates additional positive energy.

Once this energy builds, you must decide *not* to let it slow down. That is not to say that you should let your organization run abandoned, but rather continue to loosen the reins. Mario Andretti once said, "If everything seems under control, you're not going fast enough." For many businesspeople, this is a difficult concept. Most are used to managing people and departments. They have a need to feel of use, and managing provides them with that sense of purpose. You and your management team can be more productive when *not* managing and monitoring employees. Once you give your employees the responsibility and the authority to do it, your entire organization will become empowered.

By deciding *not* to engage in a conventional business format, but to instead dispense with formal policy and to provide your team with the autonomy and creative freedom to become self-managed, you will succeed in building an organization free from bureaucracy and management stagnation. Convention is the enemy of creativity, and without creativity, it's impossible to become a world-class organization. By letting go of what *used* to work, you will be focused on deciding what *not* to do. This process will become liberating for both you and your team. Your organization will be focused solely on achieving total customer satisfaction as constraints are lifted and autonomy is encouraged. This will become your brand, and your brand will keep and draw good employees. Both clients and potential employees will be drawn to your organization. Every organization's best employees want to take on responsibility. The difference with your organization is that you've built a world-class team, all hardwired for service, and it's mandatory that everyone work within a high-energy, customer-focused environment where responsibility and autonomy is celebrated and rewarded.

Before we move on to financial incentives, it is important to recognize an inherent problem when establishing world-class service: autonomy does not fit every personality. Many people already within your organization may reject this concept and the additional responsibility. Once your clients become used to receiving an above-and-beyond experience, they will not tolerate inconsistency. That is why it is important that everyone in your organization provide, at the very least, a steady and consistent customer experience. World-class standards cannot be compromised at any level. While autonomy and responsibility is desirable to high-functioning service leaders, they are not for everyone. Always pay attention for voids in the system. These voids need to be addressed and repaired quickly. Your organization's culture of service should create enough esprit de corps to either draw people in or drive them out. Be sure to consistently reward positive behavior and address any lapses. There cannot be any break in morale due to customer dissatisfaction. Everyone is working too hard in creating memorable customer experiences to be disappointed by a teammate's neglect. You must decide *not* to tolerate anything less than world-class performance. It is critical to maintain stringent guidelines around your service vision, not only when it comes to client satisfaction, but also when it comes to employee retention. The culture of service begins at the top, and it's imperative that you decide *not* to compromise your beliefs and company morale.

Financial incentives often prove to be the most difficult topic for business leaders. Many people believe that the company's financial health should come before financial incentives and distributions. While I agree with this logic, I also feel that by motivating your team with financial rewards based on performance and profits, you can achieve financial health for both your company and your employees. Several years ago, when building the business plan for my own company, I made two nonnegotiable decisions. The first was to recruit only hardwired service-oriented candidates, and the second was to hire as few employees as possible. Initially, this may seem an attempt to keep my costs low and profits high, but I was creating this business as an experiment, and after spending thirty years building experience and witnessing the collapse of service in favor of short-term profits, I decided to test a theory. After reading Jim Collins's *From Good to Great*, I decided to take a page from Nucor's playbook. In Mr. Collins's book, he describes how Nucor, a company with a struggling image and falling revenue, rebuilt themselves by hiring hardworking, self-motivated, and self-managing people. Here's the catch: their plan was to hire five employees who worked like ten, and they'd pay them like eight.

I thought this was a brilliant concept, especially when considering the enduring greatness that resulted for Nucor. Most compelling for me was the idea that with a small group of highly motivated teammates, I could spend more time building and less time managing. They managed themselves and their colleagues. There was no room for half-stepping for the employees at Nucor; either you were all in or you were out—of a job. There was every reason to insist on high standards. The selected employees were building an enduring organization while creating their own financial foundation by maintaining stringent standards, with an eye always on client satisfaction. In addition to a higher-than-average salary, the employees at Nucor also received 100 percent tuition reimbursement for every college-aged child. This was in addition to benefits and bonus incentives. The employees certainly had a lot to protect, but the real motivation came from being part of a service vision that was winning over new clients by building a nimble, customer-focused organization. I found this strategy both intriguing and compelling. Nucor was crushing its competition by providing a superior customer experience, and they were doing it with an abbreviated team of motivated employees. I had to try this model on for size.

I began to bring in new clients after establishing my company's nonnegotiable service and hiring standards and putting my team in place. This is when things got interesting. My company was fundamentally a transportation/logistic organization, and as I mentioned earlier, our service team became known for taking initiatives and creating client efficiencies. However, at the outset, there were two employees who felt overworked, while the remaining six employees felt underutilized; they wanted more work, not less. "When are you bringing in more business?" was a question I heard every day. Eventually, the two "overworked" employees moved on due to the internal pressure imposed by their more service-oriented coworkers. When I asked the high-performing employees what they thought went wrong, their answer was consistent: they did not want to be associated with people who were not willing to go the additional distance, and they most certainly were not willing to share with them in the profit-sharing plan that I had set up within the first six months of operation.

One teammate in particular was blunt in her assessment when she said, "I'm working in order to create unique solutions for my clients, and I love the recognition I receive from my coworkers and my clients. I'm not going to stand by and let someone within our organization compromise my efforts. Plus, the better the company does, the more money I make. I'm not letting anyone take money from me and my family."

Interestingly, I only replaced one of the two departing employees, and at the same time, we tripled revenue. Revenue grew because our clients gave us additional business, and word-of-mouth advertising provided us with more sales leads. In addition to altruistic motivation by way of client ownership and a higher than average salary, my teammates enjoyed the profit-sharing plan. The benefits to the organization and me were outstanding. I had a lean, efficient team in need of minimal management without the cost of a sales department. Revenue grew exponentially. In addition to creating unforgettable client experiences, every employee had an eye on profitability, and most importantly, we enjoyed 100 percent client retention. Energy was high, there was excitement around every new success, service defects were solved through a spirit of collaboration, victories were celebrated, and morale was naturally positive. This was a fun place to work and clients enjoyed doing business with us.

How you motivate your team is a matter of personal choice. I use my example as just that: an example. Clearly, finances, profits, and revenue growth are a few of the things that will dictate if and how you can roll out financial incentives. One must consider the power of ownership, both altruistically and financially, when building a world-class organization. Through ownership and empowerment you can, with very little effort, re-recruit your employees every day.

Let us take a moment to review:

- People hardwired with the service gene require autonomy. They want to own responsibility.
- Ownership comes in two forms: altruistic (client ownership) and financial.
- As a business leader, it is important to become a minimalist in your management style. The right people with the right culture leads to minimal management.
- Management should be about strengthening client relationships, not managing your team.
- The most important decisions you make are not the things you do but the things you decide *not* to do.
- Look for ways where you can financially motivate your team without risking your company's financial health.
- Encourage and celebrate creativity.

For many, this represents a profound paradigm shift in that it represents change. At first, you may feel that you are relinquishing control, but I'm suggesting that you look again at these ideas and recognize just how much control you will gain. You will have the time and resources to drive your business. You will be able to spend time with your top clients, and with their insight, you will be able to create new services and products. Employees with service aptitude will assist you in driving your organization to new heights. Most importantly, you will succeed in retaining your most valuable asset: the right people. These are high-energy, world-class, customer-focused employees, all of whom are hardwired with the very rare service gene. Re-recruiting these people becomes easier once you tap into their requisites: responsibility, ownership, creativity, and autonomy. Feed their hunger and grow your vision.

Chapter Five
LEADERSHIP: HOLDING YOURSELF TO NONNEGOTIABLE STANDARDS

> Soon the child's eye is clouded over by ideas and opinions, preconceptions and abstractions. Simple free being becomes encrusted with the burdensome armor of the ego. Not until years later does an instinct come that a vital sense of mystery has been withdrawn. The sun glints through the pines, and the heart is pierced in a moment of beauty and strange pain, like a memory of paradise. After that day . . . we become seekers.
> —Peter Matthiessen

I reference this quote often, in both leadership seminars and whenever I find myself donning "the burdensome armor of the ego." Take a moment to reread Mr. Matthiessen's quote and ask yourself, "Am I a seeker, or is my child's eye clouded over?" If you find yourself battling within the commodity marketplace, you are probably forced to work within the confines of opinions and preconceptions. Do you view every day as a battle? Do you imagine that your competitors are "gaining ground"? Do conventional business practices make you feel comfortable and safe? As you consider change, are you concerned with what other people think? And worst of all, do you listen to and repeat gossip related to your competitors? In this chapter, I'm going to challenge you to strip away all your ideas, opinions, preconceptions, and abstractions and begin leading your organization with a sense of adventure and mystery; it is up to you to create an environment where everyone is encouraged to push the boundaries of convention. The goal is to set yourself and your organization apart from the ordinary, and that can only occur by seeking new methods and practices.

I'd like to begin by defining nonnegotiable standards. While the term *nonnegotiable* conjures an image of inflexibility, I would like to suggest that the actual definition is much closer to openness and unlimited capability. The only true nonnegotiable demand is the creation of memorable customer experiences. Beginning with the creation of your culture of service, you are establishing a bedrock of creativity and transparency; everyone is encouraged to recognize opportunities where he or she can exceed client expectations. In chapter one, I described how the owner of a black-car service thought it best that his call center not waste time on calls that weren't generating revenue. On the face of it, this is a good business practice. In reality, it was one of many practices contributing to their stagnant growth. A creative approach contributed to fewer client defections and additional market share.

Most business leaders would discourage so-called nonproductive or non-revenue-producing efforts, but once you remove the burden of convention; you begin to see all client interaction as an opportunity to strengthen your brand. Tony Hsieh, CEO of Zappos, the online shoe company, tells an engaging story about a Zappos customer loyalty rep. In this story, Tony Hsieh is out on the town in Santa Monica with colleagues and vendors when, at two thirty in the morning, someone suggests ordering a pizza. Not knowing where they can place such an order at two thirty in the morning, a Zappos employee humorously suggests they call Zappos because "we understand customer service." Predictably, the Zappos customer loyalty rep informs the caller that Zappos sells shoes, not pizza. He then asks the caller to hold on for a moment, and when he returns to the line, he provides a list of five local pizzerias that stay open and deliver after two thirty in the morning.

There are several reasons why this story is interesting, but for me it's the fact that Tony Hsieh, the CEO himself, shared this story at an international summit and did so in the spirit of celebration and pride. How many business leaders do you know that would proudly share a story concerning inefficiency? What began as a middle-of-the-night prank call resulted in a living example of the Zappos brand. Obviously, Tony Hsieh is not looking through the lens of conventional business practices, and neither should you.

As you build and expand on your company's culture of service, it will become essential that you remain conscious of your own preconceptions; do not allow them to seep into your new sense of mission. Everyone within your organization will be following your lead. By challenging yourself, you will be confirming the standard set for the company. Everyone within your organization should be challenging him—or herself to always exceed customer expectations.

First, you must challenge yourself to exceed your own expectations. Become a seeker and recognize unique ways to separate yourself and your organization from the competition. One way to achieve this is to bestow greatness upon your team. By allowing everyone to achieve greatness through service you shed the "burdensome armor" of your own ego through the celebration of success. Take a moment to think about this. Within conventional business practice, the success of the organization takes precedent over individual success. In reality, the daily, individual victories create the momentum that leads to the achievement of the greater goals: client satisfaction, client loyalty, increased revenue, and a healthy, profitable organization. By celebrating individual victories and moments of greatness, you will create an atmosphere of leadership. Teammates energized by the appreciation and recognition of their colleagues will, themselves, become leaders. As you can see, the job continues to be creating positive emotional states—for your team, your clients, and yourself.

Know When To Break The First Rule

For many of you, it will be difficult to move your focus away from learned practices and procedures. You may be asking yourself, "Is it my job to insure that everyone is in a positive emotional state?" I would hope that by the time you reach this section of the book, you understand the power of emotional states. Take a moment to think back to the commodity marketplace where you and your competitors are "blanded out" by similarity. Within that landscape, both clients and employees are dulled by the process; employees come to work because they "have to," and clients purchase your product because they have a need, not because they enjoy doing business with your company. There's no electricity, no jolt of excitement. As you ponder the changes you'll have to make as a leader, consider this: 40 percent of the companies cited as being excellent in Tom Peters's book *In Search of Excellence* no longer exist. They no longer exist because they didn't change. By not changing, they became extinct. It's safe to guess that many of these extinct organizations became so because their leaders didn't see the value in changing. Being cited as "excellent" by Tom Peters became their platform and their brand, but it wasn't enough to maintain their relevance. Companies go out of business because customers don't purchase their products or services. As a business leader, it's your responsibility to create and encourage an environment where you, your team, and your organization remain relevant. And you can only be relevant if your sales are growing.

This chapter is titled "Leadership: Holding Yourself to Nonnegotiable Standards." Unlike the first two chapters, which also have *nonnegotiable* in their title, in this chapter, I did not provide a list of nonnegotiable traits or standards to which you should adhere. That is because the decision to lead with openness, trust, and enthusiasm is a personal choice. Most importantly, you have to believe in your service vision; then you have to believe in the team you've assembled, and then you have to believe in yourself and your instincts. As a customer, you recognize a superior experience and the positive emotional state it creates. Now it's contingent upon you to support an atmosphere where passion and enthusiasm thrive.

In the previous chapter, I touched upon minimizing your management style (the right people with the right culture leads to minimal management). You can support minimal management by reducing your internal vision down to its simplest level: provide memorable customer experiences. This is a difficult discipline because it requires you to return the wonder and promise of the "child's clear eye," which has been "clouded over by ideas and opinions, preconceptions and abstractions." It's difficult because no matter how hard we struggle to maintain market share and re-create our brand in an ever-changing landscape, it's inevitable that we return to the tired, old practice of business as usual. Once your organization breaks from the routine and begins focusing on total customer satisfaction, it will be imperative that you reinforce your image as the seeker. Ask questions and challenge your team to be creative and engaging as they build relationships with clients. Be sure to celebrate victories and failures. Share ideas and create a new business model; surprise your clients by exceeding their expectations; motivate your team with your wonder and promise, and be sure to surprise yourself every day by not giving in to the gravitational pull of an old, but familiar, business plan. Celebrate change; celebrate progress.

Let's review some of the proactive actions of a nonnegotiable leader:

- Be prepared to shed many conventional business practices.
- Become a seeker; look for new ways to do business.
- Maintain trust in your vision, your team, and yourself.
- Challenge yourself.

- Encourage leadership in others through the celebration and encouragement of individual victories.
- Always be aware of the emotional states of your clients, your team, and yourself.
- Bestow greatness throughout your organization.

Having been a business owner myself, I'm aware of how the daily minutia of running a business can derail momentum. Plan your daily schedule, and remain diligent in how you manage your time. With the creation of a service vision and a highly motivated service-oriented team, along with your personal commitment to become a minimalist in your management style, you should have the time to manage your business more effectively. Regardless of outside demands, remain true to your new business philosophy. You may find that your back-office business dealings will provide you with examples that you can use to enhance your vision.

In the next chapter, I'm going to relate some of the stories that led to my business vision and the creation of this book. Oftentimes, I used these examples as a means to improve existing efficiencies, or as a "Can you believe this?" moment, in order to celebrate what we were doing right. Once you make the commitment to build an enduring organization of world-class standards, every business/service encounter becomes grist for the mill. Have fun, stay focused, and remain true to your vision.

Chapter Six
"CAN YOU BELIEVE THIS?" UTILIZING EVERYDAY EXPERIENCES TO ENHANCE YOUR BRAND

> Sometimes, if you stand on the bottom rail of a bridge and
> lean over to watch the river slipping slowly away beneath you,
> you suddenly know everything there is to be known.
> —Winnie the Pooh

Do you take the time to "watch the river slipping slowly away beneath you," or do you move through everyday experiences without recognizing their value? Every day, we receive opportunities that can assist us in building airtight customer experiences. As business leaders, it's our responsibility to bring these opportunities into our own organizations; by doing so, you will create an atmosphere of awareness and insight. When building a culture of service, you'll witness your own heightened sensitivity to the varying degrees of service within your own customer experiences. Awareness and recognition to varying service levels will provide you with opportunities to improve your own service standards, thereby enhancing your brand. Consider these opportunities to be tuition-free business classes. Everyday interactions with your vendors, cable provider, auto mechanic, hair salon, and supermarket (to name but a few) become lessons from which you can strengthen your own business platform.

A few years ago, I was hired to assist an organization that was experiencing rapid growth. The owner was concerned that service levels would become diluted as they opened additional locations, and he wanted to build systems to ensure continuity. This organization's success had been built on creating memorable customer experiences. Word-of-mouth advertising had been the cornerstone of their growth. New locations would mean that individual managers were responsible for each location's profits and losses (P&L). This organization manufactured and distributed a specialty electronic product that required maintenance and upgrades. The owner was concerned that a client who purchased a product in one of his New York locations might not receive an appropriate level of service if they brought it into a New Jersey location for service. The point-of-purchase location received credit for the sale, which represented the bulk of the profit. Maintenance and upgrades produced limited revenue, and a portion of that revenue was credited to the point-of-purchase location.

In short, there was little incentive for the New Jersey location to lavish attention on a client who purchased his product in New York, and vice versa. Even though both locations "sailed under the same flag," they maintained separate P&Ls and naturally remained focused on their local customers. As I began to visit the various locations and meet with their managers, it became apparent that everyone was focused on the company's growth and success. There was no sign that clients were being treated differently based on where they purchased their product. This was a rock-solid organization where everyone was focused on creating memorable customer experiences. I began to wonder why the owner had sought my services. When we next met, I expressed my curiosity. I told him that his was one of the few organizations where I experienced almost flawless customer-service standards. I then asked him, "Why did you hire me?" His answer was remarkable.

He began by showing me his late-model Lexus, which was parked in the employee lot. "For over twenty-five years, I only drove a BMW," he told me. When his previous lease expired, he decided to lease two new BMWs, one for himself and one for his chief operating officer. At that time, his business was headquartered in Pennsylvania. He went to a local dealer and leased two fully loaded new cars. Several months later, he moved his offices from Pennsylvania to their present location in New York. That is when he began experiencing regrettable customer service. It began when he noticed that one of the tires had developed a bulge and he called a local BMW dealership to schedule a repair. He was told he would have to wait three days for a scheduled appointment. He told me that he expressed concern to the BMW representative that the tire looked unsafe. They told him that they had nothing available and that they would also have to order the tire which would take at least a day. They also informed him that they would not have a loaner vehicle available. That one phone call produced several can't dos.

Three days later, he arrived and was advised that the repair would take about an hour. He sat in the customer lounge for almost two hours before he was informed that they had ordered the wrong tire, but that they had dispatched someone to retrieve the correct tire form a nearby dealership. It was another three hours before the repair was completed. To further add to his agitation, the dealer representative informed him that they would not accept his tire/rim insurance policy because he purchased it from another dealer. Clearly upset, he presented his American Express card and was told that this dealership only accepted Visa and MasterCard. He then asked the BMW customer rep, "Are you going to allow me to leave here feeling angry?" This is the answer he received: "I put up with complaints like this all day long."

It took almost six hours to complete this basic repair. He then called the BMW salesperson in Pennsylvania from whom he had leased the two new cars. The salesperson offered no assistance, in spite of his purchase-day promise to "be here for anything you need." He called

Know When To Break The First Rule

BMW customer service and had to follow up for days before anyone called him back. He then wrote a letter to the director of customer relations at BMW asking for assistance. He explained that all he wanted was a local dealer who would provide him with a level of service that he felt he was entitled to. After he sent the letter, he received a phone call from, as he put it, "some kid who offered to send me BMW logoed valve-stem covers for my trouble." He tried a few other local BMW dealerships and was met with the same indifference. He discovered that apparently, if you lease your vehicle from one location, you're going to have problems finding a decent customer-service experience at another location. I immediately saw why he had invited me into his organization, and I was impressed with his foresight; he was determined to get his organization out ahead of the curve. Apparently, BMW and its dealerships rely on its product alone to maintain its clients' positive emotional states. Based on this story, it is as if BMW's answer to customer's complaints is: "You're driving a new BMW; that should be good enough."

Here was a business owner that used his negative experience to help strengthen his own brand. He thought, "If it could happen at BMW, it could happen here." Are you using your experiences to help redefine your customer service standards? Are you looking beyond your current success and planning for any future breaks in the system? The future is tomorrow, so use today's experiences to gain insight and strengthen your competitive advantage.

Based on his experiences, we developed several new standards that assisted in building continuity and insured client loyalty. Unlike BMW, this organization was determined to provide seamless service levels for their clients. Let's take a look at how we dissected BMW's failures to help build an airtight customer service environment for this business owner.

A glaring deficiency was the failure of the local dealership to ask the most basic question: "Why are scheduling a service appointment in New York when you leased your vehicle in another state?" By asking that one question, this local dealership would have recognized that they had a potential new client. By jumping on this opportunity to wow this customer, this dealership could have planted the seeds for a future lease and a local word-of-mouth advocate. By turning this experience around, we see a number of actions that could have been taken. First, the BMW rep should have recognized the danger of driving with a damaged tire and made an emergency appointment. If they were able to dispatch someone to swap out the incorrectly ordered tire three days later, why didn't they expedite the order immediately? You can imagine the wow factor if this client had heard, "We don't have this tire in stock, but I'll have someone sent out within the hour to pick up a new tire. Hold on while I check with the service manager; we'll work to get you in by the end on the day."

The same BMW rep also had access to this client's purchase information, which showed that he had leased two new cars. How, then, was this customer not given a white-glove experience? An alert rep (remember the service gene) would have recognized a valuable opportunity: a potential client who recently leased two new cars out of state, who now resides within one mile of their dealership and is in need of an emergency repair. It doesn't get any better than that. Why wasn't this client flagged? Upon arrival, this client should have been met by a representative and asked additional service-focused questions. They should have offered to accept payment via the insurance policy and have begun handling the paperwork while the tire was being replaced. Upon completion of the repair, the service manager should have introduced himself and provided his contact information for any future questions or concerns. In addition, by flagging this customer in their database, a personal touch could be made every time this customer called for service. It could be something as simple as, "We really appreciate that you have chosen us to be your service provider; we're well aware that you had many BMW dealerships to choose from." There is no cost associated to any of these enhancements, and yet the impact on the client is memorable.

Assuming that there will be occasional lapses in any organization's customer service systems, we then looked at BMW's safety net. Clearly, this client was looking for resolution, and all those opportunities were lost on BMW: they had no safety net. When a client is looking for resolution to a problem, they are usually saying, "I want to continue to do business with you, but I'm unhappy and need some assistance." In this instance, the client called the original salesperson and was met with something less than complacency. The salesperson leased two new cars to this client and yet chose to ignore his request for assistance. Imagine, instead, if the salesperson identified a local dealership and made a personal request that they assist this client with any future service needs. Again, the salesperson and the out-of-state dealership would have identified an opportunity to impress and thereby retain a future client. Instead, the salesperson identified a customer who had moved out of his region and he saw no value added to assisting a client to whom he promised to "be here for anything you need." Aside from a shortsighted salesperson and a neglectful customer service department, the biggest failing comes from BMW's director of customer relations. When we reviewed the letter my client sent directly to the director, I was stuck by a few phrases: "My business experience has taught me that you win your client's loyalty during times of distress"; "I have been driving BMWs for over twenty years"; and "I would like to think that BMW can provide me with a solution."

Those were the words of a customer who was looking to continue his relationship with BMW. How could anyone at BMW, let alone the director of customer relations, allow this customer to walk away without a total sense of satisfaction? BMW succeeded in creating an incredibly negative customer experience, and my client was determined to prevent his business from creating similar experiences. By peeling the onion on this experience, we developed the following nonnegotiable enhancements to his existing service standards:

- All clients are to be treated equally, regardless of their point of purchase. Your entire organization sails under the same flag.
- When dealing with an out-of-state client, utilize service-focused questions to determine any change in buying habits. Utilize this information to secure client loyalty and provide opportunities for new sales and referrals.
- All out-of-state repairs and upgrades are to be reported, on the same day, to point-of-purchase location. The point-of-purchase manager is to call or e-mail the client to extend sincere thanks and inquire about his or her service experience.
- Any lapse in service, no matter how insignificant, should be addressed and corrected. This correction should be shared throughout the organization. There should be no emphasis on blame; the emphasis should always be on service improvement.
- All complaints are to be handled immediately. Do not allow any complaint to escalate. Provide immediate remedy and follow up with the client the following day to confirm the client's complete satisfaction.
- Enter all client complaints into the company's database. This information is to be shared throughout the company via an automated efficiency (pop-up window detailing service failure). Any service deficiency is to be addressed upon the client's return. For example: "I understand we didn't meet expectations on

your last purchase. Thank you for providing us with another opportunity to restore your confidence."
- Client complaints are not to be handed off to a lower-level coworker. If a resolution becomes problematic, the complaint is to be handed up to a senior-level manager or to company ownership. This must be accomplished early in the process. The goal is to provide prompt resolution.
- Always remain cognizant that within each complaint lies an opportunity to exceed a client's expectation.

This business owner was prescient in establishing an addendum to his existing service expectations. As organizations grow and expand, service standards become vulnerable and tend to unravel. When a company decentralizes, the focus can shift away from service and onto growth. While this is understandable, it should be considered unacceptable. Standards should be analyzed and, if required, recalibrated to ensure that every customer experience remains positive and memorable.

In addition to the nonnegotiable standards listed above, this organization also looked at ways to compensate managers based on client satisfaction and client referrals. While P&Ls will always remain important, they become less important when building an organization that is determined to be known for its can-do attitude. By taking the time to watch the river slowly slip beneath him, this business owner created internal synergies that assisted his company in distancing itself from the competition and the commodity marketplace.

Every day, the river is slipping slowly beneath the bridge railing. Are you taking the time to know everything there is to be known? Every day, you are provided with examples of excellence and failure. Take time to be present in the moment. It is up to you to recognize opportunities to improve your own service vision. More than twenty years ago, I witnessed an event that changed the way I interacted with my clients when faced with a complaint. This event had nothing to do with business, but it had everything to do with human interaction. On this day, I was driving on a particularly busy stretch of the Long Island Expressway leading into Manhattan. Traffic was dense but moving at a steady forty-mile-an-hour clip when suddenly, traffic momentum halted. A young woman who was driving in the lane next to me reacted too late and hit the car ahead. What made this all the more poignant was the fact that the car she hit was a beautifully restored 1964 Mustang. What happened next was a lesson in how to alter someone's emotional state.

The young woman who was responsible for the accident sat in her car wide-eyed and anxious. She, along with all the nearby drivers, expected the driver of the Mustang to leap out of his car in an enraged state. To everyone's amazement, the driver opened the door, got out and looked directly at the woman sitting behind the wheel and asked, with genuine sincerity, "Are you all right?" The frightened young woman was stunned, and so was I. The driver of the Mustang smiled and calmly walked over to the young woman and again asked her if she was sure that she was all right. The young woman burst into tears and in between sobs said that she was sorry. The driver of the Mustang assured her that there was nothing to worry about as long as she was not hurt. He pointed to a spot on the side of the road where they could safely exchange information and then walked back to his car. Other than taking a brief glance on the way back to his car, the driver of the Mustang had not even bothered to assess the damage done to his pristine, classic car. When I looked around at the other drivers who also witnessed the accident, I noticed that they were all as astonished as I was. That whole moment was uplifting because it went against what everybody was expecting. I believe the young woman began crying precisely because she was surprised by the reaction she received.

I watched as she put her car in gear and followed the bruised Mustang over to the shoulder. As she was wiping away the tears, her face took on a look of calm and relief.

That event remained with me for several days and had occurred during a time in my life when I was closely observing successful businesspeople and looking for admirable traits that I could incorporate into my own professional personality. That one-minute exchange on the Long Island Expressway became a singular event in my professional maturity. I was impressed by how one man's sincere concern altered the emotional state of everyone within earshot. The stranger in the Mustang possessed traits that I was certain would improve and enhance most negative events. I wanted to be able to remain calm and empathetic during times of stress, mainly because I knew it would lead to more positive outcomes. I began using this approach with my clients whenever someone called with a complaint. I would begin by asking if our service failure caused any damage to their business and if so, what could I do to make it right. Instead of trying to explain how and why we failed, I focused instead on the impact our error caused on their business. I did not become defensive, nor did I become offensive. Instead, I became sincere and empathetic, which is unique when dealing with a problem. The effect was immediately positive.

By remaining calm and putting the focus on the client instead of the problem, I strengthened my business relationships and grew my business. I succeeded by being different. An otherwise insignificant fender-bender assisted me in strengthening my own culture of service. In spite of being a young and inexperienced businessman, I was cognizant that most dissatisfied customers were accustomed to having to fight for satisfaction. By taking a complaint and focusing on the effect it had on the customer, I provided myself with new opportunities. By wowing the customer with a unique approach, I diffused the problem and provided myself with opportunities to exceed my client's expectations.

You must always be looking for ways to improve yourself and your organization. Bring these lessons into your own boardroom and encourage creative improvement. When you surround yourself with people who possess the service gene, you will find yourself and your team sharing experiences that can assist you in enhancing your brand. Other than involving automobiles, the two examples I wrote about could not be more different. The first example involved an experienced businessman who utilized the failings of an international corporation to protect and improve on his own organization's service commitment. The second example focused on an impressionable young businessman witnessing a minor auto accident. While the experiences were dissimilar, the outcomes were comparable. They were used in the improvement and strengthening of a service vision.

Chapter Seven
AVOIDING SELF-SABOTAGE

> Change in all things is sweet.
> —Aristotle

Of all the ways to ruin a customer experience, self-sabotage is the most frustrating. There are thousands of examples where organizations have spent time and money on ensuring customer goodwill, only to see their efforts dashed by the effects of bad corporate policy. Usually, the offending policy was created to capture profit. Yes, I am aware that businesses must create profits, but oftentimes the zeal to drive profits can result in the loss of clients. We all know that without clients, there is no chance of long-term profits. Sometimes a new or existing policy will result in a hostile customer, someone intent on getting even. When a customer is focused on getting even, it often means that they feel cheated or robbed. I am sure we can all agree that this is not the emotional state in which we want to leave our clients.

For instance, let's review a viral e-mail that I received this past holiday season. This e-mail told a story of a shopper who purchased a GPS unit at Best Buy. The shopping experience was positive. The problem began when the shopper attempted to return the recently purchased product. He was given a refund minus $45. When he inquired about the difference, he was told that Best Buy has a 15 percent restocking fee. When he protested, he was told that this policy was printed on his receipt. How many of us read the fine print on our receipts? Should a simple purchase require us to read our receipt? I always thought that a receipt was a proof of purchase and, in turn, was the required document in the event of a return or exchange. Incredulous, he asked if he would have been charged a $300 restocking fee, had his purchase been $2,000. The answer, amazingly enough, was affirmative. The combination of fine print on a receipt along with the loss of $45 was enough to motivate this customer. He made sure that as many people as possible knew Best Buy's policy. Thanks to the Internet, word quickly spreads.

There is more to this story. The irate customer's story was being shared during the height of the holiday season. That had to hurt sales. What I found amazing was that almost every time I began to tell someone this story, they stopped me to tell me that they had already received the same e-mail. They were already aware of this story. Now, here is where it really gets gritty: this customer had taken his complaint to management and received a refund for the $45. He even stated this fact in his e-mail and yet still felt compelled to share his experience. Yes, he received monetary satisfaction, but it was too late. He remained angry and hostile. Thanks to Best Buy's return policy, the company had created, for this client, an emotional state so combustible that it continued to burn like a comet hurtling through cyberspace.

What makes this story so singular is the fact that Best Buy did, indeed, refund the offending tariff, and yet this customer remained so irate that he saw it as his duty to warn future Best Buy customers. The damage was done. Best Buy had succeeded in alienating a customer, who then made it his mission to alienate future Best Buy customers. Next time you look for ways to increase profits, make sure it is not on the back of your customers. For the record, Best Buy eliminated the restock fee in December of 2010.

Similar to Best Buy's restocking fee, accessorial fees are another method of alienating your clients. Lately, we have become accustomed to fuel surcharges being applied to airline tickets, express delivery, and taxi service. These are just a few services that have found a way to generate profits without providing any additional service. While I agree that the price of fuel has indeed affected profitability, I do have a problem when these costs are not adjusted to reflect the actual increase. Instead, an almost arbitrary percentage is being passed onto consumers. Accessorial charges do not begin and end with fuel costs. UPS and FedEx charge additional for residential deliveries. As a result, the US Post Office has seen an increase in small-package delivery. Not only does the post office not assess a charge for residential delivery; they also do not have a fuel surcharge. These accessorial charges have created a separate industry. There are now dozens of companies that provide an analysis of service failures for FedEx, UPS, and other transportation/delivery companies. These companies monitor service compliance. Should there be a service failure of any kind, these services will, on behalf of their clients, submit a claim for a refund or reduced cost. In this case, accessorial fees have created a separate watchdog industry. Clearly, the clients that hire watchdogs do so because they consider the client/vendor relationship to be adversarial.

I recently heard from a woman who was director of customer service for a regional courier service. She called to tell me that after twenty-three years, she was leaving. Apparently, as she put it, this organization had "lost its way." They had been known for, and took pride in, being different than their national competitors, such as FedEx and UPS. They had succeeded by creating a customer-centric business platform. The trouble started when their sales began to flatten and they began looking for ways to reinvent their image. One of the steps they took was to hire a new director of sales and marketing who did not have a plan to drive sales. What he did have was a plan to increase profits. His plan was to assess accessorial charges wherever and whenever possible. They assessed fees to residential deliveries, multiple-piece deliveries, and marginally oversized packages. To further add to the client's confusion, he established mileage-based pricing, which was viewed by the clients as another accessorial fee. There were other, more convoluted pricing schedules also put into place.

This woman listened as clients began calling to complain about these confusing surcharges. Management provided her with a pat answer: "These are the same fees being charged by FedEx and UPS." I am sure you can guess the customer's pat answer. It went something like this, "I'm using your service precisely because you're *not* FedEx and UPS. If you're going to begin treating me the same as FedEx and UPS, I'll begin using FedEx and UPS." Game over. Clients defected, sales and profits plummeted, morale deteriorated, and this company became a footnote within the industry. Instead of leveraging their *customer-*centric reputation, they became *company-*centric. They were no longer different than their competitors.

I am not suggesting that your organization should provide service or products at a loss. As costs increase, it becomes inevitable that prices must adjust accordingly, but your clients should never feel as though they are being nickel and dimed. In this instance, here was a healthy, profitable organization that felt frustrated by stagnant growth. They had a solid foundation upon which to build and instead, they chose what they thought to be the easiest path to increased profitability.

The fact that the clients were calling to complain about what they viewed as unfair pricing indicated that these were loyal customers who felt comfortable in their relationship with this company. What made the situation even more frustrating for this woman was that she and her team were unable to capitalize on this opportunity to strengthen the client relationship. As we should all know by now, complaints can become a portal that opens itself to dialogue. Instead of a dialogue, the customer was given a "pat" answer relating to the new fees as being consistent with industry standards. This company had previously succeeded by distancing themselves from the industry norm. That was why they had been successful. Once they made the decision to become company-centric, they lost their competitive advantage. The few clients that have remained are probably utilizing a watchdog service to capture every accessorial refund linked to a service failure. Their convoluted pricing structure has resulted in an adversarial climate. This organization has more in common with its competitors than accessorial fees.

I received a call last week from an old friend. He had just returned from a brief vacation in Florida. Instead of hearing about his vacation, I heard about his expired air miles. For more than eight years, he had been a loyal Jet Blue customer but was now flying American Airlines because when he attempted to redeem his frequent-flyer miles, he was informed that they had expired. A few years ago, Jet Blue had experienced an almost insurmountable public-relations nightmare. Jet Blue suffered a maelstrom of criticism after it was reported that more than seventy flights had been cancelled due to logistical errors. What made matters worse was that these cancellations took place as a result of a two-day-old snowstorm. In one instance, passengers had been stranded on an aircraft for more than eleven hours. In an attempt to quell the bad publicity, Jet Blue unveiled its very own passenger bill of rights. After its introduction Jet Blue founder and CEO David Neeleman went on to say, "Our airline is going to be stronger and even better prepared to serve our customers."

I guess that commitment does not apply to longstanding customers who are looking to redeem their frequent flyer miles. So here was another tale of a loyal customer defecting to another carrier. Why? It was not because of poor service; my friend had always touted Jet Blue's customer-friendly atmosphere, low cost, satellite television, easy boarding process, comfortable leather seating, and pleasant staff. He was a Jet Blue promoter. Now, he is a Jet Blue detractor. Why? Because his loyalty expired along with his frequent flyer miles. He felt cheated and decided to take his business to a competitor. Jet Blue's policy undid eight years of customer goodwill.

Hidden charges and fees, most often associated with banks and credit-card companies, have found their way into our daily lives. I am sure we have all heard someone tell us about an expired gift card or gift certificate. I was told about a Bank of America gift card that, after thirty days, began assessing monthly fees. After six months, the gift card had been reduced from $30.00 to $7.50. It appears as though Bank of America was the recipient of the gift. Our lives are filled with such examples. Each time customers are faced with accessorial charges, expired premiums, and hidden fees, there is a good chance that they will feel cheated.

Organizations run that risk, and yet they continue to nickel and dime their customers, usually because it has become an industry norm. In the example of the regional courier company mentioned earlier, they were once an organization that had succeeded by delivering a more customer-friendly experience. They delivered more than the national brands, based on their nimbleness and attention to customer needs. By creating a laundry list of accessorial charges, they became similar to their competition. The closer you get in policy and practice to your competition, the less likely your clients will remain loyal. Why should they? The same is true with the Jet Blue example. Jet Blue had, for years, celebrated their uniqueness within the industry. Its clients shared in that celebration. In fact, the company's incompetence in the aftermath of a snowstorm might have been forgiven by its loyal client base, but once it began playing by the industry's rules, it was no longer unique. Both these cases are examples where loyal customers became outraged by what they viewed as an abandonment of principles.

When building your culture of service, it is critical that you maintain your service principles throughout the entire customer experience.

Know When To Break The First Rule

If you are going to build an organization by establishing a unique experience, do not fail your clients by succumbing to the false promise associated with short-term profits. Remain unique. Remain loyal to your commitment. You owe this loyalty to your organization and to your clients.

At the start of this book, I suggested that you would be faced with the prospect of change and that the process would not be easy. In fact, it is quite difficult. As you can see from the various examples that I have provided, it has become easy for organizations to give in to conformity. Everyone else is doing it, so why shouldn't we? Accessorial charges? Let's do it! Expiring frequent-flyer miles? Yes, let's do that too! Hidden fees? Sure, let's take advantage of our client's confusion! And on and on it goes. You can choose to enter into the blandness within your industry, or you can remain steadfast in creating client loyalty through the creation of memorable customer experiences.

Chapter Eight
PUTTING YOUR CLIENTS FIRST

> Whatever joy there is in this world
> All comes from desiring others
> to be happy,
> And whatever suffering there is
> in this world
> All comes from desiring myself
> to be happy.
> —Shantideva

I struggled when outlining this chapter because I thought I might be crossing into redundancy. You could argue that this entire book is about putting your client first, and you would be correct. However, the more I thought about importance of *putting the client first*, the more convinced I became that it was important to stress this point. The reason for my determination is that today's economic climate has created an environment where customers sense that they are being viewed as victims. They have become someone to fleece. I find it amazing that as most businesses retreat into a survival mode, they have forgotten that the customer actually represents survival. In some instances, the customer is viewed as an annoyance. During tough times, businesses look for ways in which they can suck additional revenue out of their customers. On top of raising prices, many companies are using fees as a way to generate additional revenue, and there does not appear to be any end to this practice. Companies have grown accustomed to the additional profits, and consumers have become resigned.

Know When To Break The First Rule

Fees are not the only method companies use to capture revenue. Many organizations have reduced their services while raising prices. Usually, these service reductions are not announced and may, at first, be invisible to the customer. They are usually uncovered during a service or product failure, which then results in amplifying the customer's disappointment. Although consumers feel nickel and dimed, they no longer have an option when it comes to changing vendors. Each business within a specific industry seems to be following the competition.

This is a time of great opportunity. By focusing on the customer, your organization will stand above the competition. I am going to suggest that by eliminating fees for services that were once provided at no cost, you will generate goodwill, and the resulting buzz will assist you in broadening your client base. There is no better time than now to look for ways to enrich your customers' experiences. While your competitors find new ways to aggravate their customers, you should be identifying ways in which you can attract new customers. While your competitors continue to create new ways to decrease service while increasing price, you should be creating ways to increase service while decreasing price.

In the previous chapter, I discussed the adversarial aspect of the client-vendor relationship. It is important that you look carefully at your current relationships with your clients. Are you doing everything you can to ensure a positive customer experience? Let us take a look at the airline industry. I think we can all agree that it is no longer enjoyable to fly. Passengers now have to go through a tightened security process, which, in some cases, includes a full body pat down. Seating has become even more uncomfortable as airlines try to cram as many passengers as possible onto flights. You would think that airlines would be looking for ways to improve the experience. After all, travel should be a celebration of arrival and departure. Unfortunately, airlines are looking for ways in which to further damage the experience. Now, passengers are being charged for checked baggage. This has led to an increase in carry-on baggage. I don't know about you, but I truly dislike waiting in the aisle as people jam and stuff their baggage into overhead storage compartments. The result is always a delay in takeoff and disembarking. We have all stood in crowded aisles as people ahead of us struggle to take down their overstuffed bags from the overhead racks. Did anyone at the airlines think about the ramifications associated with a check-in baggage surcharge? Travelers feel so put out by the additional charge that they now look for ways to skirt the fee. The attitude becomes, "I'll show them. I'll pack as much as possible in my carry-on bag." That is some way to begin your vacation: "I'll show them." In many cases, the customer is arriving at the airport preagitated. If you understand the importance of creating a positive emotional state for your clients, then you can appreciate the absurdity in creating a negative emotional state for your clients, especially *before* they even enter your facility.

What would it look like if there was an airline that looked at client satisfaction instead of accessorial charges as a way to increase profits? Suppose there was an airline that provided swift check-in and encouraged you to check your bags instead of lugging overweight carry-on bags through the terminal and onto security belts. I know that I would welcome an opportunity to carry just a book or small computer case as I board my flight. How refreshing it would be to hear the following: "Thank you for flying ABC Air. Please allow us to take your baggage, and we will have it waiting for you when you arrive at your destination. Please just take whatever you require for your flight: a newspaper, book, or computer. You will be better able to clear security, and everyone will be able to swiftly disembark upon arrival. Allow us to make your voyage as relaxing as possible." Of course, there would be no charge associated to this most basic service.

Instead, it seems as though airlines go out of their way to create havoc and ill will. When people travel, they bring baggage. I find it interesting that an industry that caters to travelers is finding ways in which to punish its clients for bringing the very item that defines travel: a suitcase.

Clearly, airlines already have the infrastructure in place to process, load, and transport baggage. Perhaps they should look for ways to leverage the existing infrastructure to create a positive lasting impression instead of using it to alienate their customers. A wonderful example of creating customer goodwill through an existing strength can be found at any Apple retail store. One of the real hassles associated with shopping is the checkout line. At Apple stores, customers are assisted by a knowledgeable, enthusiastic sales representative. After the customer chooses the product he or she would like to purchase, the same sales rep will then, in a matter of minutes, scan the customer's credit card with an Apple iPhone and send the customer on his way. All this occurs without having to wait in line. Apple sells advanced technology, and they use their own product to strengthen their image, while at the same time, enhancing the shopping experience. This approach is brilliant in its simplicity. What would you think if Apple charged a premium for this service? What kind of emotional state would that create?

As a business owner, you can choose one of two paths. I am suggesting that by utilizing your current strengths to enhance your customer's experience, you will create more business and more profits than if you look to misuse your established strengths to create ill will. You must not lose sight of the fact that your customer's reality becomes your brand.

In the previous chapter, I stressed the importance of walking away from money-making schemes. Yes, I called them schemes, because that is how accessorial charges are viewed by your clients. You may not believe that, but I suggest that you ask your clients. I can promise you that you will not find a client in this world who feels that ATM fees, fuel surcharges, and expiring benefits are fair. Go ahead ask around. Now I am going to let you in on a secret. When you provide superior service, when you make your customer feel special and appreciated, when you create efficiencies and value for your customer, you will, in the end, make more money and more profits with less effort. You don't believe me? Well, I am going to provide you with proof, and I am going to provide you with proof that you have been ignoring for years.

Zappos achieved a 62,000 percent growth rate in less than nine years. That's right: 62,000 percent. Zappos grew from $1.6 million in sales in 2000 to more than $1 billion in 2009. How did they do it? By providing an outstanding customer experience, which resulted in incredible customer loyalty. Let us take a quick look at a few of the enhancements and efficiencies that Zappos provides for its customers. First there is Zappos' tagline: "Powered by Service" (now there's a succinct service vision). That vision created the commitment to provide "the best online shopping experience." The company achieved this commitment by taking the following actions:

- operating its fulfillment center 24-7
- storing all items in house; there is no drop shipping from outside sources
- offering free shipping (both ways, in the event of a returned item)
- "surprising" clients with shipment upgrades
- offering to pay newly trained customer service reps $2,000 to leave as a way to test their customer-service fitness

Know When To Break The First Rule

Now, ask yourself, do you see any fees or surcharges? No, you do not. In fact, Zappos is actually *spending* money in order to attract and retain new customers. Zappos experienced 62,000 percent growth without much of an advertising budget. The company chose, instead, to spend its money on creating customer goodwill. Its growth is through word-of-mouth advertising.

I'm certain that all your life you have heard, "Word of mouth is the best type of advertising." How hard do you work to create word-of-mouth advertising? Do you, instead, look to see how your competitors are squeezing additional revenue from their clients and then follow suit? While other online retailers were watching the competition, Zappos was looking for ways to exceed its clients' expectations. My guess is that your current sales exceed the $1.6 million that Zappos began with, so please do not use the excuse that Zappos is a $1 billion company. They had a vision built around the customer experience, and they remained true to their service vision. In addition to its outstanding growth, Zappos enjoys incredible client loyalty.

Earlier, you read about my experience at the Four Seasons Hotel in Santa Barbara. That experience dealt with a car valet who wowed me with a cold bottle of Gatorade. The experience I want to share now has to do with the bill I received upon checkout. During my stay, I took advantage of many of the hotel's amenities, which included bicycles, use of the beach club, and the hotel gym, to name a few. My decision to stay at the Four Seasons was predicated on a special offer provided by my credit card company. This was a four-night special offer with a price of $400 per night, with the fourth night free. This price also included breakfast each morning.

On the morning of my checkout, I approached the front desk with some trepidation. I was certain that because I had to swipe my room key each time I utilized an amenity, I was going to be surcharged to the max. Imagine my surprise when, upon receiving my bill and looking immediately at the total, I saw this: $1,200. That's right, no additional fees for any amenity, including parking. The price even included the tax. I was stunned. The price was as promised: $400 per night, with the fourth night free. I had assumed that because I was paying a promotional rate that I would be assessed every possible fee, and ironically, I would have understood. After all, I *was* staying at the Four Seasons and I was receiving my fourth night free. I was, instead, wowed by the fact that I was not being assessed any additional fees. This was on top of enjoying four days of incredible customer service, which was further enhanced by my Gatorade story. I have since returned to Santa Barbara, and I always stay at the Four Seasons. Because I am a returning customer, I enjoy an even lower per-night rate, along with preferred amenities. That's right, lower rate and additional services. They now have a loyal customer who recommends the Four Season Hotel to everyone who is planning a visit to Santa Barbara.

Neither of these companies is selling low-cost service. Zappos does not position itself as a low-cost option, and any advertisement for the Four Seasons is usually found in an upscale magazine. Both these companies are enjoying growth and profit, even during an economic downturn. How do they do it? They do it by adhering to their nonnegotiable service standards. They remain cognizant of their customers' emotional states. By putting their clients first, they remain in control of their clients' emotional states. In the example of the Four Seasons, my emotional state went from trepidation to surprise to loyalty. I have to believe that the front desk manager was cognizant of my emotional state when I requested my invoice. He is probably used to the look of surprise each time a new customer receives an invoice.

When you have put your client into a positive emotional state, you can then use this positive emotion to further enhance the experience. For instance, when the valet delivered my car complete with a cold bottle of Gatorade, I was sent over the top. Each of the steps within this process cost nothing. The Four Seasons did not incur any additional cost, and yet they succeeded in creating a lifetime customer and advocate. In the case of Zappos, their pricing is not what drives clients to their website. Their clients remain loyal because of the buying experience. I would guess that Zappos' customers are in a positive emotional state before they even pick up the phone.

Someone recently called me to share a customer story. In this instance, she had purchased a pair of children's snow boots from Lands' End in November. "I always buy a new pair of winter boots from Lands' End for my son at the start of each season," she told me. In February, she received a letter from Lands' End informing her of a problem they had "discovered." I asked her to forward me a copy of the letter, and I have to admit that I was wowed by its content. The problem had to do with a cosmetic issue (in some cases, the color peeled off) that did not "affect the performance or protection of the boot." Lands' End considered this problem "unacceptable" and offered a full refund of the purchase price. In addition, the letter offered a 25 percent discount on her next Lands' End purchase. Take a moment to process this. Lands' End did not wait for their customers to call and complain. Instead, they got out ahead of the issue and offered a full refund. The boots had been purchased in November and they were now offering a full refund in February. In addition, they were extending a 25 percent discount for this customer's "trouble." This woman's loyalty to Lands' End was validated when she received this letter.

Lands' End did not suggest a prorated refund. They chose to eliminate any potential ill will by offering a full refund *and* a 25 percent discount on a future purchase. What would you have done if you were Lands' End? Would you have waited for your clients to complain before offering a refund? Would you have even offered a full refund three months after the purchase, or would you have tried to negotiate? Lands' End made a decision, which had a monetary cost. They made a decision to put their clients first, and by doing so, Lands' End enhanced their brand.

What each of these organizations sell is value, not price. As a result, they do not have to charge fees, or apply surcharges. Their clients remain loyal because they are confident of receiving value. In addition to receiving a great customer experience, they are assured that the price offered will be the price charged. How refreshing. Price becomes irrelevant when you provide world-class service. World-class organizations do not nickel and dime their clients. They rather spend their time finding ways to exceed their customers' expectations. These organizations have found ways to avoid pricing complaints by focusing on their brand.

Is your organization customer-centric or company-centric? Are you putting your clients first, or are you putting short-term profits ahead of your clients? How focused are you on maintaining the customer experience? I can promise you that by focusing on the customer, you and your team will have more fun. Wouldn't you rather your meetings be focused on exceeding customer expectations? Imagine, if you will, opening each meeting with, "How can we blow our competition out of the water? How can we wow customers away from our competition?" Regarding profitability, allow your accounting department to tell you what you need to charge in order to remain profitable. Do not waste time looking for ways where you can profit from your customers' confusion. Leave that to your competition. Let them bleed their customers with fees. If you remain loyal to your commitment to service and integrity, your competitor's "bleeding" customers will become your customers.

Chapter Nine
REMAINING TRUE TO YOUR VISION

> Pray to God, but hammer away
> —Spanish proverb

At this point, you have either bought into these concepts or have dismissed these ideas as unrealistic You might be saying to yourself, "Zappos, Lands' End, and the Four Seasons are large, robust organizations and they possess enough resources to spend money on the creation of memorable customer experiences." For those of you who have dismissed these concepts as unrealistic or unattainable, I would like to suggest that you already possess the resources needed to build a culture of service. You have to begin by viewing your organization from a different angle. Only then will you identify the opportunities available to you. For those readers who recognize the power and focus within the customer service vision, I have to guess that you have already indentified ways in which you can leverage your existing resources. It could be as simple as empowering your best employees to create memorable customer experiences. It may also require you to take your best people and put them on the front line. This could result in some restructuring, but your long-term vision must dictate your actions.

Last year, I provided consulting services for an organization that supplied medical supplies to hospitals. This organization was experiencing client complaints due to shipment discrepancies. The problem was a result of a disconnect between the call center and the warehouse. In short, the call center was promising what the warehouse could not deliver. In spite of the internal pressure, I always found Tripp, the warehouse manager, and his team upbeat and energized. Both the call center and the warehouse took these complaints seriously and without rancor. They looked for solutions and deployed new software to alleviate the problem. The customer service reps and the warehouse personnel were professional and always customer-centric in their approach. In the end, there was just too much inventory that required special packaging due to fragility, hazardous material, and oversized equipment. This resulted in some shipments being delayed. When we questioned the customers regarding their frustration, it became apparent that the delay was not the problem. The problem was the confusion created by the lack of product knowledge. There was, however, someone who possessed knowledge around product and packaging constraints. In addition, this person had great communication and leadership skills. This person was the warehouse manager, Tripp.

Senior management took the unusual step of promoting their warehouse manager to director of customer service. This would be considered radical except for the fact that Tripp was universally respected by his colleagues and possessed excellent communication skills. The call center reps quickly embraced the idea. The results were remarkable. Within six months, every customer service representative was thoroughly educated in packaging and shipment limitations. Tripp bridged the communication void that had previously existed. With Tripp at the helm, customer expectations were being exceeded thanks to internal symbiosis. The existing customer service software was scrapped in favor of a customized program. Tripp and the customer service team worked directly with system programmers and created an automated solution unique to their marketplace. This approach was effective because the warehouse and customer service departments were working together in the same room. As a result, customer complaints dropped by almost 70 percent.

By the end of the year, Tripp's job description was again changed. He now acts as a liaison between customer service and sales. In his new role, Tripp is a point man who meets regularly with customers and creates new service efficiencies specific to client needs. As a result, client retention and sales have increased. In this instance, management recognized that their weakest link existed between customer service and the warehouse. That single, weakened link resulted in client pain. Instead of replacing the link, they strengthened it by taking a knowledgeable, customer-focused employee and utilizing his talents to improve and then enhance the customer experience. Tripp possesses the service gene and before his promotion, his talents were being underutilized. This approach is brilliant in its simplicity because it utilizes existing talent that might otherwise be wasted.

Do you have a Tripp hidden somewhere in your organization? Have you identified the employees in your organization who possess the service gene? Are you leveraging their talents to strengthen your service vision? Chances are, you already possess the talent needed to take your organization to the next level. In the example I just used, this company did not increase its costs in order to separate themselves from the competition. Senior management recognized Tripp's strengths and abilities and took a chance by moving him into a higher-profile position. This single change created a competitive advantage, but this organization did not stop there. As soon as the internal communication link was repaired and strengthened, management looked for another way to rise above their competition. By sending Tripp out in to the field to meet with customers, they were better able to understand their clients' needs. This provided them with new opportunities to exceed their clients' expectations. Remaining true to your vision requires creativity, diligence, and perseverance. You must quickly adapt and advance when faced with any deterioration in service.

Exceptional service soon becomes expected service. That is why you and your team must always be looking for ways to improve and expand the customer experience. Many organizations rely on technology as a means of providing efficient service. There is no denying that technology will continue to have a profound effect on the way we do business and how our customers shop. The inherent risk with technology is that it can disconnect your clients from the human side of business. In the example I just used, Tripp and the customer service team assisted in building an automated system that mirrored human efficiencies along with customer expectations. It was effective because it spoke directly to their client's needs, while leveraging internal efficiencies. To further enhance the customer experience, Tripp was deployed to meet directly with the customers. They reinforced their automated improvements with personal relationships. Technology should be used as an enhancement, not as a replacement for customer connection. You should utilize emerging technological trends as a means to remain competitive, but do not rely on new technology to create a positive emotional state for your clients. That can only be accomplished through personal connection.

Final Chapter
THE BEGINNING

> Simplicity is the most difficult thing to secure in this world; it is the last limit of experience and the last effort of genius.
> —George Sand

Now it is time for you to begin exacting the change necessary to create an environment where a culture of service will define both you and your organization. While the concepts I've discussed are simple, putting them into practice will prove difficult. By now, I have made it quite clear in stressing the difficulties associated with change. I have not provided you with any difficult concepts. It is quite simple: make your customer feel special. This is accomplished by adhering to the most basic of life's lessons. You have heard these words resonate throughout your life: "Do unto others as you would want done unto you." It is also referred to as the Golden Rule. It is a simple rule, and yet most business leaders become so focused on profit that they lose sight of their responsibility to their customers, their employees, and to themselves.

An antagonistic environment will result in customer defection. As customers depart, most organizations find themselves having to scramble to replace lost profits, and they attempt to do so by repackaging themselves. Unfortunately, this repackaging ends up being more of the same because they resort to following trends within their own marketplace. Most business leaders follow their competitor's lead. While it is important to make adjustments to remain competitive, it is imperative to create efficiencies that elevate you above your competition. The question you must always be asking yourself is, How can I distance myself from my competition? As I have been discussing in this book, the best way to increase your competitive edge is by establishing a superior customer experience. Considering that most products and services are similar, your success will be determined by your uniqueness. Through the creation of memorable customer experiences, you will stand out within a marketplace defined by *sameness*.

You should have an understanding of nonnegotiable service standards and the importance of creating a culture of service. By now, you should be attuned to recognizing people who are in possession of the service gene. Hopefully, when purchasing a product or service, you are categorizing and rating your own customer experiences and utilizing them to enhance your clients' experiences.

In the previous chapter, I urged you to reject accessorial fees, surcharges, and reduction of service as a means of capturing additional revenue and asked you to focus instead on creating memorable customer experiences. I understand how difficult it is to give up short-term gain for a long-term vision. I used the regional courier company as an example of short-term gain resulting in long-term loss. In that example, a small company had succeeded precisely because it had been different from its larger competitors. The company built its reputation by exploiting the service void created by the national brands. In their attempt to mirror the big boys, they became irrelevant. If you believe that by raising your customer service standards you will separate yourself from your competitors, then it is critical that you maintain these standards throughout the customer experience.

Prior to the start of any new policy, you should ask yourself and your team, "How will this affect our customers' experiences? What effect will this have on our customers' emotional states?"

Once I began this project, I found myself inundated with customer service experiences. Almost every day, I received at least one phone call or e-mail detailing either a wonderful or dreadful customer experience. I heard from many businesspeople who had become dialed in to the customer experience and began utilizing their experiences to help redefine their own organizations. A few of those stories found their way into this book, but the real benefit to me was the reassurance that I was on to something. Thanks to these shared experiences, I remained motivated. Anyone who has ever written a book or taken on a large project will understand the power of encouragement. Each story was a gift that assisted in propelling me forward with this project.

The title of this book, *Know When to Break the First Rule,* came from a personal experience. I was a young college student looking to make extra money, and I was referred to a restaurant owner who was looking to hire a bartender. During my first day on the job, the owner sat me down and explained his two rules of bartending. The first rule was to never buy a customer a free drink. The second rule was to know when to break the first rule. In a split second, I understood everything I had learned about customer service up to that point. His rules were simple yet brilliant. There were no rules. The only rule was to make sure that every customer left his establishment in a positive emotional state. He was granting me autonomy and trusting my judgment. Everything that I had learned about customer service up to that point crystallized before my eyes. Could it really be that simple? I spent the remainder of that first day behind the bar thinking about the Two Rules. Yes, I decided, it was that simple.

Every business has rules. It is important to have rules; otherwise, there would be anarchy, theft, waste, and lack of productivity. However, it is more important to ensure client satisfaction, and how could you better impress and surprise an unhappy customer than by breaking a rule? When you are given the authority to break a rule, you are given the power to create positive emotional states. This is real power. When

I was told I could break the first rule, I was given ownership. I was responsible for my customer's emotional state. I was in charge. Rules are important, but autonomy is more important.

During my time as a bartender, I learned a lot about customer service. I learned how easy it is to turn a bad experience into a memorable experience. I learned that few professions prepare you better for a customer-centric mindset than being a waiter or waitress. In a single restaurant, you will encounter more people with the service gene than in any other business. I also learned that if you do not possess it, you will not last in the restaurant business. If the customers do not chase you out, your coworkers will. I learned that the best waitstaff always put their customer's emotional state ahead of anyone else's, including their own. Their tips depend on it as much as their integrity demands it. I learned about the power of teamwork. Any break in service usually results in a customer becoming dissatisfied. Everyone swims or sinks together.

Standing behind the bar, I would sometimes survey the dining room and marvel at the ballet of efficiency: busboys hustling and cleaning tables, waiters and waitresses leaning over menus explaining dish preparations to the diners, water glasses being filled, food being served, wine bottles being uncorked, and fresh silverware being laid out between courses. Everyone was dialed into the same channel: the customer channel. And what made this frequency special was that whenever we lost the channel, we all had the authority to dial it back in. We all had the power to *break the first rule.*

My bartending job was another semester in my customer service education. I began my studies as a twelve-year-old paperboy. It was a job that required me to know and use every customer's name. It was a job that taught me about the importance of customer satisfaction. It became the foundation upon which new lessons and observations adhered. And as this foundation strengthened I became even more convinced that a sincere customer-centric approach to business would all but eliminate price based competition. Early in my career, I learned that world class service renders price meaningless.

Last year, I returned to the old neighborhood to attend a funeral. A friend's mother had passed away. After the funeral, we gathered at a restaurant for dinner. During dinner, I noticed an elderly woman sitting across the table staring at me. She looked vaguely familiar, but I couldn't place the face. It seemed as though every time I looked up, she was staring at me. Finally, I smiled and introduced myself. When she told me her name, I remembered her from my newspaper route. "You lived at 8819 193rd Street," I said. She smiled broadly and said, "That's right, and I remember you as well. You were our best paperboy."

About the Author

As the founder and principal consultant of The McConnell Group, Joe McConnell has built and realigned customer service divisions for many organizations, large and small. He's a strong proponent of creating a seamless environment where all employees enjoy and take part in providing a superior client experience. Joe believes, and has proven, that a total customer service experience is achievable and essential in building an enduring organization.

www.ingramcontent.com/pod-product-compliance
Lightning Source LLC
Chambersburg PA
CBHW030847180526
45163CB00004B/1487